In Search of Stonewall

In Search of STONEWALL

The Riots at 50
The Gay & Lesbian Review at 25

Best Essays, 1994–2018

Edited by Richard Schneider Jr.

G&LR Books
Boston, Massachusetts

G&LR Books
PO Box 180300
Boston, MA 20118
HGLR@aol.com

In Search of Stonewall / Richard Schneider Jr. — 1st edition
ISBN: 978-0-578-41108-8

Dedicated to the more than 1,300
writers who have contributed to
THE GAY & LESBIAN REVIEW / WORLDWIDE
over the past 25 years

Contents

In Search of Stonewall

RICHARD SCHNEIDER JR.

THE year was 1994. It was the 25th anniversary of the Stonewall Riots and, as luck would have it, the year in which a new magazine called *The Harvard Gay & Lesbian Review* was publishing its first issue (Winter '94). The "Harvard" was dropped in 2000 and "Worldwide" added, but other than that *The G&LR* has had an uninterrupted run of 136 issues over the past quarter-century. The fact that our first year coincided with Stonewall's 25th proved a happy coincidence, if only because it gave us something important to talk about that year. But it also joined our fate with that of the founding event of the modern LGBT movement. This book commemorates our own 25th birthday with a collection of Stonewall-related articles selected from the issues published to date.

I've chosen the title "In Search of Stonewall" for this collection because it seems to me that the events of 1969 remain elusive in at least two ways. First, there is the journalistic question of just what happened on the night of June 28th (who started the riot, what happened next, etc.). Second, because "Stonewall" exists as a symbol of the LGBT movement quite apart from the historic event itself, the search is always on for the meaning of Stonewall as it was first conceived and as it has evolved over the years. If nothing else, it is a marker in historical time with a clearly defined "before" and "after." But to imply that Stonewall interrupted the flow of history, single-handedly resetting the LGBT calendar, is to pile a lot of responsibility onto a single event or era. Still, something happened, and it happened quite rapidly and even magically after the riots, so in this sense the search for Stonewall can also be a desire to reconnect with the overpowering energy and excitement of this period.

The sequence of events following the riots—the founding of new gay organizations, new publications, the first Pride parade in

June 1970, and so on—are indeed a breathtaking slice of history. The question of *why* Stonewall became the symbolic birthplace of the modern LGBT movement has been raised, sometimes with considerable passion, by many people who point out that the West Coast is where the movement really began, way back in the 1950s, complete with organizations and magazines and even riots long before 1969. The fact that it took New York City to spark a national movement undoubtedly has more to do with that city's sheer size and dominance of the news media, especially at that time, than to a lack of passion or organizing savvy on the West Coast. (Also, let's face it: "Stonewall" is a damn good name for a popular struggle. What if the riots had happened at Uncle Charlie's?)

What distinguished the early movement as it fanned out from New York was a new emphasis on "coming out" about one's sexuality to family, friends, and anyone who would listen. California groups like the Mattachine and the Daughters of Bilitis were secretive organizations whose members largely hid their identities. The concept of coming out as a personal imperative was clearly a prerequisite for a mass movement, which is by definition a public undertaking. Feminists and leftists at the time exhorted people to see the personal as the political. LGBT people had no choice: the decision to come out as gay—especially when homosexuality was illegal—was an intrinsically political action.

The Stonewall Riots have often been compared to the Storming of the Bastille in 1789. It's a fair comparison, however much they differed in size and scale: both were collective acts of resistance against an oppressive establishment; both demonstrated the power of numbers and the possibility of fighting back; and both gave rise to a movement for which this founding event became a rallying cry. For the LGBT rights movement, having a symbolic starting point has been especially important. Unlike the Civil Rights Movement, which was assembled and sustained by charismatic leaders like Martin Luther King, Jr., the LGBT movement never really produced a central figure to personify its goals. Stonewall provided not only a founding event but also an anniversary to celebrate each June.

THIS book is organized into four sections comprised of articles from *The G&LR*'s first 25 years. Here is a rundown of some of the burning issues addressed by our many illustrious authors.

The stature of Stonewall as a mythical starting point might be expected to render the details of the riots themselves inconsequential. No one cared that the Bastille housed only a handful of prisoners. And yet, the question of what took place on that June night, and above all who participated, has never been settled to everyone's satisfaction and seems to be gaining in urgency. Most of the attention has centered on the demographic question of who was present at the Inn—what was the ethnic mix, the ratio of drag queens to working-class youths, etc.—and who threw the first punch or the first brick. It matters because the presence of the various constituents of this LGBT+ coalition of ours at the movement's founding has come to be seen as a mark of legitimacy. These lingering controversies, among others, will be taken up in PART I of this book. In addition to the eyewitness accounts, several pieces address the age-old question of why Stonewall "caught on" and created a revolution while earlier events did not.

Just as the Storming of the Bastille was preceded by years of skirmishes and pamphleteering that should have tipped off the monarchy that something was afoot, Stonewall—or rather the explosion of organizing and protest that followed—was the culmination of two decades of conscientious efforts to pull a "homophile" movement together, most of them on the West Coast, as the articles in PART II reveal. Harry Hay, founder of the Mattachine Society in L.A. in 1948, is often credited as the first gay organizer, with Del Martin and Phyllis Lyon not far behind with the Daughters of Bilitis. There were even some riots at gay bars in San Francisco and L.A. in the 1960s, though they never reached the scale of Stonewall. Meanwhile, on the East Coast, Frank Kameny and his posse were demonstrating peacefully in front of government buildings in the 1960s. It would be hard to argue that these efforts led directly to the riots of '69, but organizations like the Mattachine are what morphed into the far more radical groups, such as the Gay Liberation Front, that now emerged.

What happened right after the riots, the subject of PART III, made all the difference in the formation of a viable mass movement. Here it's worth noting that "Stonewall" became a touchstone for gay resistance soon after the event itself, and indeed the effort to create a symbol was quite deliberate on the part of early leaders (notably Craig Rodwell). What solidified the symbolism was the choice of a date for New York's first gay pride parade to coincide with the first anniversary of Stonewall. Why the early gay liberation movement adopted the very radical agenda that it did can only be understood in the context of the times. The riots occurred during the same summer as Woodstock, which might be seen as the high water mark of the Counterculture of the 1960s and '70s. The Civil Rights Movement of the '50s had given way to Black Power; the antiwar movement was colossal and growing; and the Women's Movement was becoming an all-out Sexual Revolution. No doubt it was the latter to which the LGBT movement owed its closest allegiance and its early success. For if premarital sex was suddenly fair game after centuries of prohibition, not to mention divorce and serial monogamy and hitherto unheard-of sexual possibilities (see *The Joy of Sex*), why not same-sex relations and identities? Indeed the early gay movement took its place at the head of the Sexual Revolution, calling for a complete rejection of puritanical restrictions in favor of an ethic that allowed consenting adults to engage in sexual relations regardless of gender, marital status, number of participants, or whatever.

The radicalism of the early movement pretty much guaranteed that its center of gravity would drift toward moderation over time. Inevitably, some people would charge that the revolution had been betrayed. This magazine started publishing amid a lively public debate over the future of the movement, with one side arguing that we should just admit that the revolution was over and embrace a more modest agenda of acceptance into mainstream society, the other claiming that all was lost if that's what the LGBT movement had come to. Several articles in Part IV comment on the strategic shift that was taking place at this time (the early to mid-1990s) from the old "sexual liberation" model to one of "identity politics." Two decades later, another group of articles observe—and mostly lament—that precisely this kind of assimilation into mainstream society has occurred. We may have earned our "place at the table"—we can now get married and serve in the military—but the vision of true liberation, of a universal acceptance of sex and gender difference and diversity, remains elusive. These goals will apparently have to wait for the next revolution.

PART I

Flashpoint: New York City, June 1969

One of the few extant photos of the rioting at Stonewall in late June, 1969.

Stonewall's Challenge to Historiography

MARTIN DUBERMAN

WRITING gay history is no less perilous than writing any other kind. "Objectivity" is the professional historian's golden calf, but as we know, that prized possession proved elusive—a false idol. Historians necessarily base their accounts on the always fragmentary, partial evidence that *happens* to have come down to us from the past.

The inescapable limitations of historians themselves—the idiosyncratic experiences and values they often unconsciously hold—inevitably shape their interpretations, further distorting our ability to know "what actually happened." If postmodernism has taught us anything, it is that subjectivity is omnipresent in historical narration. No matter how scrupulous the historian is, the evidence will always remain incomplete, the portrait tainted—and historians themselves will always, inescapably, interpret the past through the distorting lens of their own times and preoccupations. "Objectivity" remains the ideal goal, but like all ideals it can only be approximated, never achieved.

Thus it is with regard to the events at the Stonewall Inn in 1969. The vast majority of those who directly participated in the rioting, or observed it from the sidelines, have never been asked for or offered their versions of what took place. Among the small minority who have borne public witness, accounts vary—sometimes crucially.

One persistent view credits a butch dyke with striking the first blow; another insists on awarding the garland to a drag queen; a third assigns it to one of the street kids who hung out in the park adjacent to the bar. One "authoritative" account has it that the cross-dressing rebel Sylvia Rivera first threw down the gauntlet; another counters that Sylvia was never even present at the riots. A prominent theory about the corrupt Sixth Precinct's uncharacteristic failure to alert Stonewall's Mafia owners to the imminent raid ascribes it to the owners' tardiness in the making their usual payoff. An opposing theory emphasizes instead that the Precinct's new commanding officer was sending a message that henceforth the payoffs had to be higher—or, argues yet another theory, that he was determined to abolish them altogether. And so it goes.

The six commentators who describe the events at Stonewall in the following section make honorable attempts at completeness, and none directly contradicts well-established outlines of the rioting. Yet each chooses to highlight aspects of the event that—for whatever subliminal reasons—best suit their subjective snapshot. In turn, I myself am drawn—for reasons no less subjective or unwitting—to favor certain emphases in one account over another. Thus I prefer the way Michael Denneny references the 1960s context in which the Stonewall riots took place—and particularly the Women's Movement—to the way in which David Carter minimizes the importance of the pre-Stonewall homophile movement, insufficiently acknowledging the extraordinary bravery of that tiny, intrepid band in publicly protesting their odious treatment.

Finally, though, I'm most taken with Toby Marotta's central emphasis on Stonewall as "a disorganized rebellion against oppression," yet one that "triggered a chain reaction of community-building and political organizing that was emulated across the country and publicized throughout the world." Understanding that, I'd agree, is more important than knowing whether the first or the third night of the rebellion was the bloodiest—or whether Sylvia was or was not sleeping off a hangover.

October 2018

What Went Down

TOBY MAROTTA

IN the wee hours of Saturday June 28, 1969, a team of plainclothes police detectives raided the Stonewall Inn. "The Stonewall" was a gay bar located close to where Christopher Street meets Seventh Avenue in Greenwich Village. Across the street from it stood a roughly triangular sliver of land named Christopher Park. This sparely landscaped, fenced-in oasis was an island in the storm of cross-cutting streets, sidewalks, subway entrances, and bus stops that kept Sheridan Square busy day and night.

On the night of this June 28th bar raid—the most recent of several such incidents at the Stonewall Inn and other gay haunts in "the Village"—authorities followed their standard procedures. First they released bar patrons able to show the proof of legal age they were required to carry. Then they escorted apprehended bar employees and men presumed to be dressing as women to police vans waiting in the street to transport them to the Sixth Precinct police station. Here these cross-dressers would be examined to verify that they were men, and all designated law-breakers would be booked and arrested.

This night, however, most of the dislocated patrons had refrained from fleeing into the night. Instead, they were loitering on the sidewalk alongside the park, watching the rest of the proceedings unfold. When some of the presumed cross-dressers tangled with the officers who were escorting them to the curb, members of this impromptu audience broke another precedent by shouting encouragement. When someone managed to jump out of a van and run off, they cheered. Passersby attracted by the commotion joined in.

Led by a few precocious activists, several of these observers began to taunt the police. Soon they were pelting them with coins, rocks, bottles, and bricks. When the stunned detectives retreated into the bar, the result outside was surprise and delight, followed by a surging sense of power at having challenged and intimidated long-feared authority figures. Emboldened protestors now swarmed across the street, crowded onto the sidewalk in front of the Stonewall, and bashed in its windows and doors.

Police reports recorded this episode as a "riot" that lasted for forty minutes. Officially it ended when a summoned squad of riot-control police succeeded in clearing the stretch of Christopher Street in front of the bar. Despite erected barricades and posted patrolmen, however, agitated and awestruck spectators milled around in Sheridan Square, the bulk of which lies on the far side of Christopher Park, until daybreak.

As far back as the 1920's, Greenwich Village had been known as a bohemian enclave whose residents included prominent homosexual artists and intellectuals. By 1969, so many of the district's residents and visitors were gay, and so many of its commercial establishments gay-oriented, that the Village effectively functioned as a gay ghetto. Yet even as gays grew more comfortable in this neighborhood, it was customary for them to play it safe and act straight when in public, avoiding physical contact. Few of those who now descended upon Sheridan Square had ever before bared their homosexual feelings outside private or anonymous settings.

All day Saturday, as word spread about the previous night's rioting, their numbers continued to grow. Gay visitors examined the battered façade and boarded-up windows and doors of the Stonewall Inn. They gathered across the street in and around Christopher Park to gossip, share impressions, and speculate on what might happen next. By the afternoon, the Stonewall had reopened as a juice bar. Its employees were handing out balloons. Its owners, well into their third year of profitable operation, were blaming the police for the raid. But already they, too, had been put on notice that there was a new force in town—what the eye-catching graffiti chalked onto their storefront called "Gay Power" and "Queen Power."

As evening arrived, friends greeted one another and even newly identified acquaintances with shameless hugs. Improvised wisecracking, singing, and dancing gave rise to more choreographed cheers, chants, and kick lines. For the first time, in-group slang, campy performance, unspoken lusts, and even long-suppressed resentments were being aired—all this in an officially patrolled public place.

As midnight came and went, more and more bar hoppers joined these lingering festivities. Soon partisans of every openly GLBT stripe had engulfed the entire eastern end of Christopher Street, extending from Seventh Avenue down two long blocks to where Greenwich Avenue meets Sixth Avenue, commonly known as the Avenue of the Americas. Now this row of charming apartment houses and arty shops was closed to traffic.

Once again, siren-screeching, light-flashing vans emptied squads of riot-control police into Sheridan Square. Wedges of these masked, shield-carrying, baton-and-tear-gas wielding officers worked to clear the occupied stretch in front of the Stonewall. Others used the same strong-arm tactics to drive hordes of jubilant people from the corner of Greenwich and Sixth Avenue. But here, too, their efforts to herd revelers and stymie their high jinks created a manic mix of challenge, defiance, evasion, and escape. As on the night before, these street-clearing efforts spurred scores of agitated rioters to escape into accessible side streets and circle back via other entrances to Sheridan Square.

This second night of rioting was both more antic and more purposeful than the spontaneous outburst of the night before. It was accompanied by more tangles between officers and gay people. It resulted in more violence and greater bloodshed. And it led to incidents of individual and organized acting-out that filtered into the surrounding neighborhood and continued until the dawn of Sunday June 29.

A heavy police presence kept agitators in check for the remainder of Sunday. Rain discouraged visitors from congregating in Sheridan Square on Monday and Tuesday evenings. But on Wednesday, July 2, after dark, the bloodiest and most destructive rioting of all flared up on this easternmost stretch of Christopher Street. At one point there were blazing fires in all of the steel trash containers that lined its sidewalks.

THIS whole wave of disruption, from the three nights of street demonstrations to the countless acts of resistance and defiance by these characters and cliques, would soon be dubbed the Stonewall Riots. It started as a disorganized rebellion against oppression, but it triggered a chain reaction of community-building and political organizing that was emulated across the country and publicized throughout the world. Overnight this unprecedented surge of organizing transformed what had been a largely underground vanguard movement into a highly public mass movement for gay pride, power, and community.

Exactly one year later, at the end of June in 1970, representatives of these newly organized and mobilized subgroups came together to commemorate the Stonewall Riots with a week of what were dubbed Pride Events. Their climactic Sunday march and "Gay-In" were billed as the "First Birthday of Gay Liberation." And the designation stuck: we still celebrate Gay Pride in June and count the years since Stonewall. In just one year these activists and community builders had founded new organizations, notably the Gay Liberation Front and the Gay Activists Alliance, radical groups by today's standards but the start of an institutionalized national GLBT rights movement.

For all the drama of the riots themselves, it's clear that the significance of "Stonewall" lies in what the riots immediately precipitated in the summer of 1969: an unprecedented surge of activism and organizing for gay and lesbian rights. They empowered a new generation of activists and engendered a whole new approach to gay and lesbian politics.

The first night of rioting in front of the Stonewall Inn is still mythologized in much the same way that the French have mythologized the storming of the Bastille in 1789—an incident to which it is often compared. To be sure, there had been similar riots in other cities, notably Philadelphia, San Francisco, Los Angeles, going back to the mid-1960's, so this style of "rebellion" was already out there in the popular consciousness. What differed in New York was not the spontaneity of the first night but the increasingly organized efforts that followed on successive nights—and above all the more sober organizing that followed once the riots had ended.

A Report from the Front

EDMUND WHITE

I wrote this letter to Alfred Corn, who would go on to become one of the leading poets of my generation, and to Amy Jones, at that time his wife (she would become an important Renaissance scholar in comparative literature). Alfred and Ann (to whom I dedicated Forgetting Elena*) were among my closest friends. They had been living in Paris for a year when I wrote them. Alfred was quite open about being bisexual, so I knew my letter would fall on friendly ears.*

The letter is not entirely accurate and the tone is rather frivolous—signs of how lightly even the participants took an event they had no idea would become historic. Stonewall took a while to transform us all; I wrote this letter to entertain before the transformation had taken place.

— Edmund White

July 8, 1969
Dear Ann and Alfred,

Well the big news here is Gay Power. It's the most extraordinary thing. It all began two weeks ago on a Friday night. The cops raided the Stonewall, that mighty Bastille which you know has remained impregnable for three years, so brazen and so conspicuous that one could only surmise that the Mafia was paying off the pigs handsomely. Apparently, however, a new police official, Sergeant Smith, has taken over the Village, and he's a peculiarly diligent lawman. In any event, a mammoth paddy wagon, as big as a school bus, pulled up to the Wall and about ten cops raided the joint. The kids were all shooed into the street; soon other gay kids and straight spectators swelled the ranks to, I'd say, about a thousand people. Christopher Street was completely blocked off and the crowds swarmed from the Voice office down to the Civil War hospital.

As the Mafia owners were dragged out one by one and shoved into the wagon, the crowd would let out Bronx cheers and jeers and clapping. Someone shouted "Gay Power," others took up the cry—and then it dissolved into giggles. A few more prisoners—bartenders, hatcheck boys—a few more cheers, someone starts singing "We Shall Overcome"—and they started camping on it. A drag queen is shoved into the wagon; she hits the cop over the head with her purse. The cop clubs her. Angry stirring in the crowd. The cops, used to the cringing and the disorganization of the gay crowd, snort off. But the crowd doesn't disperse. Everyone is restless, angry, and high-spirited. No one has a slogan, no one even has an attitude, but something's brewing.

Some adorable butch hustler boy pulls up a parking meter, mind you, out of the pavement, and uses it as a battering ram (a few cops are still inside the Wall, locked in). The boys begin to pound at the heavy wooden double doors and windows; glass shatters all over the street. Cries of "Liberate the Bar." Bottles (from hostile straights?) rain down from the apartment windows. Cries of "We're the Pink Panthers." A Negro queen whirls like a dervish with a twisted piece of metal in her hand and breaks the remaining windows. The door begins to give. The cops turn a hose on the crowd (they're still within the Wall). But they can't aim it properly, and the crowd sticks. Finally the door is broken down and the kids, as though working to a prior plan, systematically dump refuse from the waste cans into the Wall, squirting it with lighter fluid, and ignite it. Huge flashes of flame and billows of smoke.

Now the cops in the paddy wagon return, and the two fire engines pull up. Clubs fly. The crowd retreats.

Saturday night, the pink panthers are back in full force. The cops form a flying wedge at the Greenwich Avenue end of Christopher and drive the kids down towards Sheridan Square. The panthers, however, run down Waverly, up Gay Street, and come out behind the cops, kicking in a chorus line, taunting, screaming. Dreary middle-class East Side queens stand around disapproving but fascinated, unable to go home, as though torn between their class loyalties, their desire to be respectable, and their longing for freedom. Sheridan Square is cordoned off by the cops. The United Cigar store closes, Riker's closes, the deli closes. No one can pass through the square; to walk up Seventh Avenue, you must detour all the way to Bleecker.

A mad left-wing group of straight kids called the Crazies is trying to organize the gay kids, pointing out that Lindsay is to blame (the Crazies want us to vote for Procaccino, or "Prosciutto," as we call him). A Crazy Girl launches into a tirade against Governor Rockefeller, "whose empire," she cries, "must be destroyed." Straight Negro boys put their arms around me and say we're comrades (it's okay with me—in fact, great, the first camaraderie I've felt with blacks in years). Mattachine (our NAACP) hands out leaflets about "what to do if arrested." Some man from the Oscar Wilde Bookstore hands out a leaflet describing to newcomers what's going on. I give a stump speech about the need to radicalize, how we must recognize we're part of a vast rebellion of all the repressed. Some jeers, some cheers. Charles Burch plans to make a plastique to hurl at cops.

Sunday night, the Stonewall, now reopened—though one room is charred and blasted, all lights are smashed, and only a few dim bulbs are burning, no hard liquor being sold—the management posts an announcement: "We appreciate all of you and your efforts to help, but the Stonewall believes in peace. Please end the riots. We believe in peace." Some kids, nonetheless, try to turn over a cop car. Twelve are arrested. Some straight toughs rough up some queens. The queens beat them up. Sheridan Square is again blocked off by the pigs. That same night a group of about seventy-five vigilantes in Queens chop down a wooded part of a park as vengeance against the perverts who are cruising in the bushes. "They're endangering our women and children." *The Times,* which has scarcely mentioned the Sheridan Square riots (a half column, very tame), is now so aroused by the conservation issue that it blasts the "vigs" for their malice toward nature.

Wednesday. *The Voice* runs two front-page stories on the riots, both snide, both devoted primarily to assuring readers that the authors are straight.

This last weekend, nothing much happened because it was the Fourth of July and everyone was away. Charles Burch has decided it's all a drag. When he hears that gay kids are picketing Independence Hall in Philly because they're being denied their constitutional rights, he says: "But of course, the Founding Fathers didn't intend to protect perverts and criminals." Who knows what will happen this weekend, or this week? I'll keep you posted.

Otherwise, nothing much. I've been going out with a mad boy

who tried to kill me last Friday. He's very cute, and I'm sure it'd be a kick, but I think I'll take a rain check on the death scene.

Finished the first act of my play and outlined the second. My sister has a new boyfriend who's got $30 million, two doctorates, working on a third. She met him in the bughouse (shows the advantages in sending your daughter to BEST bughouse in town). I'm going out to Chicago in two weeks to help her move.

I miss you both frightfully. No more fun dinners, no endless telephone conversations, no sharing of exquisite sensations, gad it's awful.

Love, Ed

Marchers entering Central Park at the first Pride parade in New York City, June 28, 1970

Stonewall as Event and Idea

MICHAEL DENNENY

AS we celebrate the 25th anniversary of the Stonewall riots, much is being written about that now mythical event which is generally taken as the birth of the contemporary gay and lesbian rights movement. Much of what I have read strikes me as wrong-headed, especially the revisionist attempts by the currently politically correct to downplay the role of white males in that event. "Middle class white men" is the term generally used, but considering the reputation of the Stonewall, or just glancing at the few photos left from that time and place, one wonders about the term "middle class"; one wonders about the word "men." "Randy white boys" might be more accurate. Recently I read a manuscript proposal (generated by a PBS television series on gay rights) that asserted that "middle class white men" had "stolen" (their word) Stonewall as an event, appropriating to themselves an action generated by lesbians, transvestites, and people of color. The authors offered no evidence for this statement, just blandly asserting this revision of history with the same smug and self-righteous certainty that Stalin's encyclopedists must have felt as they dutifully revised their history decade after decade.

Personally, I doubt that the Stonewall, while clearly a racially mixed bar, was ever a popular dyke hangout, or that its clientele was anything like equally divided between men and women. And while anyone who knew Marsha or Sylvia knew what a force Street Transvestite Action Revolutionaries (their term) could be in a confrontation with the cops, the contribution of either to the ongoing organizing of the gay movement is a different question.

But, in retrospect, all these squabbles to claim credit are not only petty but beside the point, except when they interfere with the attempt to ascertain historically what actually happened. They are beside the point because they misunderstand how an event like Stonewall actually comes to interact with history, becomes a part of history, or not. Stonewall was not the first time gay people had confronted the police, nor the first time we stood up for ourselves. John Preston once told me about a gay bar in Chicago a year or so earlier. The police were harassing the owners and made the patrons walk a long gauntlet of cops while being photographed entering and leaving the place. For the people involved, this confrontation was as harrowing and as heroic as Stonewall, but it had no echo across the country and is now almost forgotten. There had also been a similar confrontation in L.A.

So what made Stonewall different?

Kant wrote of the French Revolution that it was not so much the rioting that was going to change the world as the quality of attention paid to it by spectators, by those observers across Europe who watched the unfolding events in Paris and came to believe that something momentous had happened. It was what the spectators made of the events of the French Revolution that would change history, not what the rioters in Paris had done. In other words, it is when an event is raised to the level of an idea that it has the power to alter history through the consciousness of people.

I would argue that something similar is the case with Stonewall. It was definitely not the first sign of the emerging gay revolt. A year-and-a-half before Stonewall, a couple of guys had started *The Advocate* in Los Angeles, at about the same time that Troy Perry had established the first of the Metropolitan Community Churches, today the largest gay organization in the world. Clearly, something was afoot with gay people even before the events at Stonewall. What was missing was any sense of possibility, any alternative, to the oppression gay people faced daily everywhere they looked.

To get a sense of the mental oppression our people labored under, this lack of possibility that was so spiritually suffocating, one might look at Mart Crowley's play *The Boys in the Band*, a much maligned work that precisely delineates the pre-revolutionary emotional situation that would lead to Stonewall. The play is about eight gay men and one straight; in essence, the gay guys, who are very unhappy and bitchy, start the evening beating up on each other and progress till their anger is directed at the straight man. What is amazing in this play is that none of the gay characters has any sense of possibility, any way out of the trap of gay life as it was then led. Although they are clearly angry to the point of fury, the idea of gay liberation is the furthest thing from their minds. As someone who remembers the years before Stonewall, I can testify that the very concept of gay liberation would have then struck most of us, even those of us who were intensely politically active, as absurd. Being homosexual was a psychological situation, maybe a medical situation, but certainly not a political matter.

Luckily for everyone, the women's movement came along and got us to consider the notion that the personal *was* political: a major step forward. Then what was needed was a crystallizing moment, and the five continuous nights of rioting that the raid on Stonewall provoked offered that moment. What was decisive was not the event itself, but how people responded, the immediate, spontaneous and utterly decentralized flurry of organizing, leafleting and pamphleteering that resulted (and which was so well documented in Donn Teal's 1972 book *The Gay Militants*). It was this response, and perhaps above all the late Craig Rodwell's determination to commemorate the event the next June with the world's first Gay Pride March, that made Stonewall the shot heard 'round the world.

The event had become an idea, the idea that gay people would fight back, would stand up for their rights. And ideas are what change the world.

The Remains of the Night

FELICE PICANO, TOM BAKER, RITA MAE BROWN,
MISS MAJORS, VICTORIA ROTH, AND EDMUND WHITE

DURING the many 25th anniversary celebrations of the Stonewall Riots in 1994, I was somewhat surprised to hear so many people saying they had been there that night in June, 1969. I remember once adding them up and concluding that if everyone who said they were there, actually had been present, that they not only would have taken over Sheridan Square completely, but possibly taken down the municipal government of New York City altogether.

We all want to be part of something historic; it's human nature. And let's face it, there really haven't been that many truly positive and exulting events for LGBT people to want to absorb and make their own. Usually we're commemorating a death, a disease, something awful. So possibly these hundreds of people mean that they took part in the demonstrations that occurred in and around Sheridan Square on the nights and days following that first night, when gays fought back against the police raiding a bar in Manhattan. And let's remember there had been raids of gay bars before in which people fought back in one way or another—in Los Angeles, San Francisco, and even in the small town of Pacifica, California.

But for some reason, this particular incident stuck, with the result that a routine bar raid developed into something far larger. A new minority came together in the weeks that followed, and out of that arose an active political movement. First came the Gay Liberation Front, which would be followed by the more active and successful Gay Activist Alliance. Today, we can trace the LBGT political movement in the U.S. back to that one night. We recognize it as, in effect, the Big Bang that created our gay universe.

I realize that these days "history" itself has become a suspect and at times even a moot item of terminology. Like others I've heard that histories are "what the winners tell you it is" and that "everyone has a different idea of what a historic events is" and other such truisms. While granting all that, I still believe that trying to discover what actually happened is not a worthless enterprise. True, many who were at or around the Stonewall that night are missing or dead. But others, like myself, are still alive, and over the years some people who happened to be in, at, or in the vicinity of 35 Christopher Street have been generous enough to tell me of their experience. In addition, for this essay, I've been lucky enough to hear from other people I did not know, who were in, at, or near the bar that night—their strong voices speak for themselves.

I'm always a writer, which means that I'm also often a journalist. So here is my Journalism 101 attempt to get at the truth about Stonewall. My "sample" includes three gay men, a transgender person of color, a lesbian, and a heterosexual woman who lived a few doors away—which I think pretty much matches the population of the area that night. The witnesses are, in alphabetical order: Tom Baker, Rita Mae Brown, "Miss Majors," Felice Picano, Victoria Roth, and Edmund White.

Some background on my interlocutors:

§ Tom Baker worked for years for Grey Advertising in New York and Los Angeles on the Ford account: he was for a short period of time a bartender at the Village gay bar Julius'; since retiring, he has written and published two books relevant to the Stonewall period, *The Sound of One Horse Dancing, Full Frontal,* and *Paperwhite Narcissus.*

§ Rita Mae Brown is the celebrated author of the groundbreaking lesbian novel, *Rubyfruit Jungle,* as well as *Six of One,* both of which deal with that early period of feminist-lesbian America; she is also the author of many beloved mystery novels.

§ Miss Majors is a transgender African-American woman who now lives and works in Oakland California.

§ Victoria Roth is a classical pianist, chamber musician and music teacher.

§ Edmund White is the renowned author of novels, memoirs,

plays, and biographies, including the memoir *My New York* and the novel *The Beautiful Room is Empty*, both of which deal with this era. My own books relevant to 1960s New York include the memoirs *Men Who Loved Me* and *True Stories: Portraits from My Past*.

I've asked these five people, and myself, five basic questions. 1. How did you happen to be there that night? 2. What did you think was happening at the time? 3. Did you have any idea that history was being made? 4. What did you think in the days after it happened? and 5. Does any detail stand out for you, even now, years later?

— *Felice Picano*

How did you happen to be there that night?

Rita Mae Brown: I was walking at home with a friend. We did a newsletter for a feminist group of the time called "Redstocking" (i.e. radical Bluestockings) in a building near NYU. It may have been the same building as the Shirtwaist Factory fire that killed so many young women workers many decades before. We were headed to my little hole-in-the-wall apartment at Charles Street in the West Village, and Christopher Street was my usual crossing place.

Edmund White: I was just walking past Sheridan Square with my close friend Charles Burch the night of the raid. I had stopped going to the Stonewall because it had been taken over by drag queens, whereas before it had been a simple gay cruise bar where people danced to jukebox tunes.

Tom Baker: I had just moved to New York after being released from the Army and was living in a sublet, rent-controlled apartment at 72 Barrow Street. I had just started my job as a media trainee at Grey Advertising making $5,000 a year. I was also still pursuing my acting career, going to auditions, and working with the newly formed Roundabout Theatre Company with Gene Feist. That night I was out walking the streets looking for a quick blow job.

Miss Majors: I'd had a tough day and I heard that that singer Judy Garland had died. I wasn't a fan of hers, but I didn't feel like being alone, so I went down to the Stonewall. That was our club, where the other T's and I could hang out and relax and be ourselves. Sure, there were gay boys there and some dykes. But it was an easy mix, and that's where we used to go. It was tough being a transgender person and a black person in those days, tougher than today. And a lot of us were "working girls" too—you know, hustling, but I'd been working at the Jewel Box Revue as a dancer.

Viki Roth: I'm willing to tell you what I remember from that night. The dinner to which my husband Gene's father and his wife had been invited was at our apartment at 45 Christopher Street. I think it was their first time visiting us in our new apartment, and I remember Gene's father asking about the neighborhood, which we loved. Nice restaurants, food shops—the original Jefferson Market and Balducci's, and all the great little shops along Bleecker Street, and a phenomenal record shop on Eighth Street that was open evenings until way past midnight.

Felice Picano: I'd been invited to a birthday party of a friend of a friend: James Mathis, a concert pianist from Texas (I think) who lived on the south side of Sheridan Square opposite the Stonewall. I met my pal Joseph Mathewson, who lived on Hudson and Jane Street, and we walked down to Christopher Street. It was a nice summer night and we noticed a lot of people out and around, but as we went into the party, it seemed like any other typical Saturday night in the Village.

What did you think was happening at the time?

RMB: We'd passed the Stonewall and had reached Seventh Avenue when we heard the police sirens. We were waiting for the light and we saw the police go into the bar. We figured that it was the usual "clean up" by the vice squad. You know, the cops would go into a bar and take people out in a paddy wagon. Back at the police station they would call up their lawyer buddies to come arrange bail. A corrupt system was in place. It was a real racket.

EW: We could tell it was a raid, since there was a "Black Maria"—a paddy wagon—out front on Christopher Street. Once it was filled, it took the detainees off (mostly the bar staff and belligerent drags) and some cops stayed behind until it returned.

MM: Well usually when there was a raid, the police would be outside the place hitting the door jambs with their sticks. You would hear that and you would know to move away from another person if you were too close or something. But that day just didn't go down right at all. I'd been at Sing Sing [prison] before that, and the "girls" there had told me that if I ever got into a confrontation with a cop, I should do something small like swear at him or spit in his face. That way he'd knock you out with his nightstick instead of them all beating you up and injuring you for life. So when I heard one of the "girls" outside the bar screaming and then I heard a big crash like glass breaking, that's what I did. I spit at this cop and he knocked me out. I don't remember a thing after that. I woke up in a paddy wagon.

FP: I was on the top floor in the back of the building and had no idea anything at all was happening at the Stonewall Bar or Sheridan Square. Jimmy was playing piano, people were drinking and smoking grass and singing and making a lot of noise. I'd just met the cute bartender and decided he would be my date that night. Someone who left earlier than we did came back upstairs and told Jimmy something. But if it was about the raid, I never heard it.

RMB We saw the police go in and then we saw the police come flying out again, being pushed out by the people inside the bar. It was at night, and that area was tree-lined and badly lit, so we couldn't actually see who was fighting the police. All we could make out were figures; it wasn't clear if they were guys or transgender people. But right away we knew that they weren't being docilely rounded up as usual. They were fighting and screaming, and then more and more people started coming out of the bar. We got out of there in time to see some guys trying to tip over a Volkswagen that was parked on the street.

By the time I came back to Sheridan Square, there were wooden police horses set up and police paddy wagons and police cars. They'd cordoned off the area, so you couldn't get near. So I walked around and over to Sixth Avenue, where the Women's House of Detention was. Word must have reached them to, because the noise coming out of there was incredible and it was clear that they were rioting too.

VR: What we witnessed was upon exiting our building to get a taxi to take his father home. It was always hard to get a cab in front of 45 Christopher, so we would walk over to Sixth Avenue. As we walked down Waverly Street, there were phalanxes of police in riot gear, making their way to Christopher Street—and to Stonewall.

TB: I came across all this commotion on Seventh Avenue. Sheridan Square was mobbed with people and police in riot gear. It was very noisy and chaotic, and I could only get to see from the outer fringes of the crowd.

MM: I don't remember a thing after that cop knocked me out. I actually think it was those hustlers, those young white boys that used to hustle out of Sheridan Square Park, who initiated the provocation. They'd be out there every night, and they were troublemakers. Only they didn't stick around, because I didn't see any of them being arrested.

Did you have any idea that history was being made?
VR: Not at all. When we got back to our building, we weren't able to get in—I think we were kept on the other side of Sheridan Square. Later in the evening, we were permitted back into our building. I don't recall how long the wait was, but in addition to police, I recall there were also fire engines and ambulances.
EW: Word of mouth spread quickly that the cops had raided a gay bar. We were angry because earlier in the 1960s Mayor Wagner had constantly raided gay bars in an effort to "clean up" the city for the World's Fair. But we thought those days were over, and we considered Mayor Lindsey a liberal, although he was a white shoe Republican and an enemy of organized labor. I returned to Sheridan Square the next two nights, where there was a growing demonstration, some violence. The police cordoned off Sheridan Square for a while. So, yes, I did think history was being made. But a funny, ironic revolution. When we would chant "Gay is Good" in imitation of "Black is Beautiful," we would all laugh. When we called ourselves the Pink Panthers in an echo of the Black Panthers, we were just being silly.
RMB: No, it took me a good year or two to see that my brothers were not backing down, not going back to the old way. I sort of got a hint of how that evening sort of became like nuclear fission when I saw its effect on the women's House of Detention. That gave me hope.
MM: I didn't know at all. You know it was hard enough being a transgender black person and trying to get through the day and pay the rent without bothering to think about politics. So the significance was lost on me and on most of the other "girls" at the Stonewall too.
TB: I knew it was a raid of some sort but had no idea history was being made. I was, if anything, a distant observer, not a demonstrator. And, as I recall, I did not get my blow job.
FP: Not until the next morning. I was awakened by a phone call

from friend Douglas Brashears, who had not been at the party, though he'd been invited, and he wanted to know if I and the others had been arrested, and I said no. Then Douglas said something odd for him. He was the loudest and funniest and femmiest guy in our set, but he got really serious and said, "The queens have begun revolting. And they aren't going to stop now."

What did you think in the days after it happened?
RMB: Stuff would be happening around Sheridan Square each night. I would dip in and dip out to see what was going on. Before that, we had been trying to organize women at the bars. We were what people later called the "Lavender Menace" of the Women's Movement. But a lot of gay and lesbian people even in the Village were content with their duplicitous lives. They'd made their peace with that. But once the Stonewall riots happened, people sort of woke up, including women.
EW: Although I was basically a middle-class prig, afraid everyone would go too far, even I felt a strange exaltation. What changed that night was that gays, who'd long thought of themselves as a sin, a crime, or an illness, suddenly saw themselves as a minority.
MM: Nothing then. But a year later I heard that there was going to be an anniversary parade for the Stonewall raid, and I wanted to know what that was all about, and I went there not bothering to get all dressed up [as a woman].
FP: We went down there the next day and people were protesting as close as they could get to the bar, which was still blocked off, so they were out in the streets off Seventh Avenue and at the subway station exits, handing out flyers that read "We're not going to take it anymore!" Monday evening there were a half dozen guys at each of the four station exits walking around with posters and megaphones, shouting "What Do We Want?" To which people would answer: "Gay Rights." Megaphones: "When do we want them?" Crowd: "Now!" Any one coming out of the subways would instantly be in the center of this protest. Some would leave and others would stay and join. These protestors were all gay guys around my age, including some of my friends. I joined them and if I knew someone coming by. Over the next week, it became the place to go to hang out and meet people. As in: "See you at the protest tomorrow; then we'll go have dinner."
EW: Revolutions are always started for the wrong reasons in less

than ideal circumstances. The Boston Tea Party was tax resisters; when the Bastille was stormed there was only a handful of prisoners in it. The Stonewall was an unhygienic Mafia bar that battened on our oppression. No matter, it was one of the first times we didn't run away from the cops.

Does any detail stand out for you, even now, years later?
TB: The one vivid image I remember was that of a parking meter that had been ripped out of the sidewalk.
RMB: We saw guys picking up a Volkswagen parked on the street and trying to overturn it. We left then because it seemed pretty violent. I always wondered what happened. That was such an extraordinary sight.
VR: Those phalanxes of police in riot gear, making their way up to our little Village street!
EW: The sound of inmates in the women's prison at the Sixth Avenue end of Christopher Street banging their tin cups against the bars and shouting their encouragement to the rioters.
FP: Coming out of that building two hours or so after the riot had happened, the bartender and I thought we were hallucinating. Sheridan Square was transformed and almost unrecognizable. There were large black NYPD busses all around the square blocking it off from other streets. There were wooden "horses" set up inside the park itself like a maze. You couldn't see the Stonewall at all. There were wood panels over the window and doors. The place was filled with policemen and firemen in full gear. Everywhere you stepped there were big black fire hoses snaking along the ground. There was a Volkswagen knocked over onto its back. A taxicab was halfway up a fire hydrant. It had knocked the cap off and water was gushing twenty feet into the air. Stepping out of the building, we were immediately escorted by cops over to Seventh Avenue and told to go up to Bleecker Street, as the area was closed off. We couldn't figure out what happened. It was like a meteorite had hit or something equally catastrophic.
RMB: I leave you with the words of my mother: Make Hell with what you have.

What Made Stonewall Different

DAVID CARTER

IN the forty years since the Stonewall Rebellion, an event that achieved legendary status almost before it was over, its power as a symbol has continued to rise more or less unabated. Four decades later—after two books, one film, several radio documentaries, countless articles and news stories; after hundreds of gay events and organizations named in its honor; and after becoming the first gay and lesbian site to be designated a national historic landmark—Stonewall retains its power to fascinate and inspire. On this anniversary both the BBC and PBS are making their first documentaries about the Stonewall Riots. It is therefore worth considering why Stonewall became such a ubiquitous symbol.

The place to start is the context in which the Stonewall Riots occurred. The perception that homosexuals had it hard before Stonewall is often accompanied by the belief that the further one goes back in time, the worse the situation for gay people was. If it was bad in the 1960s, imagine how much worse it must have been in the '50s, the '40s, and so on. But historians have shown us that this is far from the case. William N. Eskridge, Jr.'s 2000 book *Dishonorable Passions: Sodomy Laws in America* demonstrates that colonial and American sodomy laws were written not with homosexuals in mind but with an entire range of nonprocreative sexual acts. Legal records reveal that the main categories of persons charged with sodomy were those who had sex with animals or used force to have sex with others, especially women and children. It was only in the late 19th century that sodomy laws started to be written with homosexuals in mind.

George Chauncey's *Gay New York* (1994) disclosed that a thriving gay subculture existed in New York by the early 20th century. This subculture was sufficiently tolerated that it burst into the mainstream popular culture in the 1920s and '30s as the "pansy craze," which in turn created a measure of gay visibility in films and plays. However, a backlash began during the Depression era and worsened during World War II, culminating in the cultural nightmare that was the 1950s. David K. Johnson's *The Lavender Scare* (2004) shows how the terror brought on by the Cold War fed a national hysteria about homosexuality. In the end it was homosexuals, even more than Communists or their sympathizers, who bore the main brunt of government purges. In 1953, Carlisle Humelsine, the security officer for the Department of State, testified before Congress that out of 654 State Department dismissals or forced resignations on security or loyalty grounds, 402 were for homosexuality. Johnson estimates that the number dismissed on suspicion of being gay during the McCarthy era would eventually rise to some 5,000.

The association of homosexuality with Communism coincided with a hardening of the American psyche during the Red Scare, which engendered a corresponding desire for American males to be "tougher." The hypermasculine male ideal that emerged in the 1950s wreaked havoc on the image of gay men. Sex offender laws were revised in the '40s and '50s to stiffen penalties against homosexuals and to allow for their involuntary commitment to mental institutions. Once institutionalized, they were subjected to a ghastly range of "cures" that included chemical and electric shock treatments, castration, and prefrontal lobotomy. Religious organizations were unanimous in their condemnation of homosexuals—completing what homophile activists like Frank Kameny and Barbara Gittings saw as a triple condemnation that left no escape for homosexual citizens. The law condemned them as criminals, medicine declared them insane, and churches branded them as sinners.

In *GayLaw* (1999), Eskridge summarized the litany of such laws and policies that were in place by the '60s:

> The homosexual in 1961 was smothered by law. She or he risked arrest and possible police brutalization for dancing with someone of the same sex, cross-dressing, propositioning another adult homosexual, possessing a homophile publication, writing about homosexuality without disapproval, displaying pictures of two people of the same sex in intimate positions, operating a lesbian or gay bar, or actually having oral or anal sex with another adult

> homosexual. The last was a serious felony in all states but one [Illinois], and in most jurisdictions also carried with it possible indefinite incarceration as a sexual psychopath. ... If the homosexual were not a citizen, she or he would likely be deported. If the homosexual were a professional ... she or he could lose the certification needed to practice that profession.

This assault on lesbians and gay men explains why the self-image of homosexuals was so negative at this time. The minds of gay people had been so colonized by the heterosexual world that almost no one could imagine a positive gay identity, let alone a positive gay culture. Thus homosexual rights as a political cause—except for the extremely rare gay person who participated in the homophile movement—would not have occurred to most gay people, even those who were very politically engaged. For example, Danny Garvin, who in 1969 lived in the only gay commune in New York, often talked with his fellow commune members about the war in Vietnam and women's rights, but they never had a single political discussion about homosexuality.

Michael Denneny had been very politically involved since the late 1950s, when he was a teenager. He had sat in at the Woolworth counter in Providence in sympathy with the sit-ins conducted to protest segregation in the South and was thrown out of his high school for starting a front organization for Women Strike for Peace. When he went to the University of Chicago, he helped edit *The Hawk and the Dove* magazine, showing that in 1964 he was among the very few Americans who publicly questioned whether the United States should be in Vietnam. Still, he had never considered his homosexuality from a political perspective. "Homosexuality was so heavily psychologized that the idea of looking at it through a political lens just didn't occur to me."

When my friend Donn Teal, author of *The Gay Militants* (published in 1971), died last February, I examined his papers. Among his documents I found an envelope filled with the dozens of letters he received when he wrote the first article ever published in *The New York Times* by a person who self-identified as gay. The article, titled "Why Can't 'We' Live Happily Ever After, Too?" published less than five months before the Stonewall Riots, criticized films, plays, and books for not providing positive images of gay people. What was so remarkable about the letters that he received in response was that whether they were written by people who identified as lesbian, gay, or straight, the vast majority of the letters criticized the article for being shrill and overstating the case: things surely weren't as bad as all that in the arts! The "kulturkampf," as Eskridge called the antigay clampdown, was so complete that the American populace, both gay and straight, could not think seriously about gay oppression.

There were other stirrings of gay awareness in the '60s, to be sure, but organizations like the Mattachine Society for gay men and the Daughters of Bilitis for lesbians were practically secret organizations—if only because the media refused to cover their activities—while their publications (*ONE* and *The Ladder*) were essentially *samizdat*. However, it is precisely because the American public was so unaware of these early stirrings that the Stonewall Riots came as such a shock to the system. Michael Denneny, living in Chicago, remembers his reaction on seeing a headline about rioting homosexuals in a New York newspaper: "Stonewall came like a thunderclap."

To be sure, Stonewall had its precedents in the form of a few rumbles in gay venues in L.A. and San Francisco and a protest or two in Philadelphia and Washington, DC. Some have suggested that Stonewall doesn't deserve the special status it has acquired. But as interesting and important as those other acts of resistance are—and as courageous as those who protested were—this still does not give them the historic weight of Stonewall. Compared to these earlier events, Stonewall was of a different order for four reasons: it was the only sustained uprising, lasting six days; it was the only one that involved thousands of people; it was the only one that got much media coverage; and it was unique in engendering a new kind of militant organization (first the Gay Liberation Front and later the Gay Activists Alliance) as well as a new political ideology known as "gay liberation." It also does not stand to reason, as some have argued, that Stonewall was "bound to happen" or that it was some kind of fluke. There were certainly many raids on gay bars before Stonewall, and even some violent resistance in cities like L.A. and San Francisco, but the fact remains that they did not generate a sustained mass uprising.

In researching my book on Stonewall a few years ago, I recorded many firsthand stories that illustrate what a shock Stonewall was to the collective gay nervous system.* Take Robin Souza, who was traveling on the New Jersey Turnpike to Philadelphia with two straight female friends on the night of June 27, 1969. As they listened to a rock and soul station, Robin and his friends were amazed when a newscast announced that gay men and the police were fighting a pitched battle on the streets of Greenwich Village. Although Robin imagined a battle waged with guns, he felt impelled to turn the car around and head for the Village to witness what was happening. In far-off South Vietnam, a gay Army man assigned to watch over the news ticker on Saturday, June 28th, was reading reports on the tickertape as it streamed out when it suddenly ran out of paper. He continued reading until he reached the tape's final words, "Homosexuals riot in Greenwich Village," and he received one of the biggest thrills of his life. In Long Binh, Vietnam, U.S. Army Specialist 3 Henry Baird sat eating lunch in the mess hall and reading a military newspaper. As he scanned the day's news summary, his eye was drawn to a short paragraph that described a riot led by homosexuals against the police in Greenwich Village. He told radio producer David Isay, "My heart was filled with joy. I thought about what I had read frequently but had no one to discuss it with. Secretly within myself I decided that if I should survive to come back stateside I would come out as a gay person."

In San Francisco, a gay man who had just heard news of the riots in one of the city's gayest areas watched in amazement as he witnessed the news physically spreading. As one gay man would approach another on the street and start telling him the news, more men would cluster around and listen, the group would break up, and each in turn would speak to the next man he ran into, the news spreading like a nuclear chain reaction. In a convent owned by the Sisters of Charity, a nun of Italian descent heard the news over a radio in her room. She had entered the convent determined to work out the moral meaning of her lesbianism. She had just turned 29 after three years of celibacy when the news coming over the radio made her suddenly realize that she was not alone. "It hit me with a bolt of lightning. It was as if I had an incredible release of my own outrage at having to sequester so much of my life. To me, it was the quintessential 'enough is enough.'" A few weeks later Virginia Apuzzo left the convent to start a new life. When Joan Nestle heard of the rioting she went down to the Village on Saturday, June 28, and stood in the street in front of the Stonewall Inn, looking at the police barricades and the crowds that had gathered.

"There is a background to what happened in that bar, a building up of rage like volcanic steam, over the years. I remember standing there and knowing that a new time had come because that rage had exploded."

Several of these individuals would go on to play a leading role in GLBT activism and scholarship. Michael Denneny packed up his belongings and moved to New York to figure out what it meant to be gay. His exploration eventually led to his founding, with Chuck Ortleb and a few others, the influential literary magazine *Christopher Street*, where many of the Violet Quill writers first published their works. Later, Denneny founded the nation's first gay imprint, Stonewall Inn Editions, at St. Martin's Press. Robin Souza, using the pseudonym Gary Dutton, became one of the founders of the Gay Activists Alliance, the organization most responsible for the spread of the gay liberation movement that emerged from Stonewall. Joan Nestle founded the Lesbian Herstory Archives, and Ginny Apuzzo became the executive director of the National Gay and Lesbian Task Force before she became an advisor to President Bill Clinton.

The sum total of the changes brought about by the Stonewall Riots transformed the small homophile movement into a mass movement, as summed up by Frank Kameny, an activist in Washington, D.C., for years before Stonewall happened: "By the time of Stonewall, we had fifty to sixty gay groups in the country. A year later there were at least 1,500. By two years later, to the extent that a count could be made, it was 2,500. And that was the impact of Stonewall."

Immanuel Kant famously wrote of the French Revolution that "The occurrence in question does not involve any of those momentous deeds ... of men which make small in their eyes what was formerly great. ... We are here concerned only with the attitude of the onlookers as it reveals itself in public while the drama of great political changes is taking place." In other words, the fall of the Bastille and the French Revolution had the impact they did because of their effect, not on those who participated in these events, but instead on those who witnessed them. It was the same with Stonewall: the event derived its power from the emotional shock it created in those who heard about it.

One thing that's rarely acknowledged in our gauzy memory of the Stonewall Riots was the critical role of violence in the event.

Observed Denneny: "I was struck by the fact that more cops ended up hospitalized than demonstrators. That made an impact on me. I think it was decisively important that there was physical violence, that gay people fought back, and that the riots went on for several nights. I think had they been peaceable and gone the way of all the civil rights demonstrations that were happening in the 60s, I don't think it would have had the same impact at all." Just as nonviolence allowed African-Americans to overturn the racist image of blacks as violence-prone and achieve a measure of moral superiority, the use of violence by gay men subverted the stereotype of homosexuals as ineffectual and lacking in courage or masculine qualities.

Stonewall became an overnight symbol but could easily have faded as new events unfolded in the Gay Liberation movement. What gave it staying power was Craig Rodwell's flash of insight when he got the idea to memorialize the riots with an annual celebration. Since June of 1970, when the first marches were held to celebrate Stonewall in New York, San Francisco, Chicago, and Los Angeles, the idea of holding an annual march has spread to other cities around the U.S. and eventually around the world. Notable are marches that occur in countries where homosexuality is still harshly condemned, such as Russia and Croatia, whose governments have tried to stop the marches. Marchers are sometimes attacked by skinheads and the like, often with the complicity of the government, and forced to fight back. Thus the militancy and sometimes even the violence of Stonewall continue to be recapitulated in such places, where rights are far from won—which is to say that Stonewall continues to serve as a symbol of gay rebellion and liberation.

The Making of *Gay Liberation* (the Statue)

DAVID B. BOYCE

IN June of 1994, the modern Gay Liberation movement marked its 25th anniversary in New York City. Attending the festivities in Central Park's Sheep Meadow on that bright and hot summer day, I watched as hundreds of thousands of people gathered to listen to speakers who extolled the years of progress since that June night of a quarter-century ago. After several hours in the park with friends, we made our way through the crowds to head downtown and see what was happening in the Village.

Christopher Street was like an open-air subway car at rush hour, so we took a breather in Christopher Park, across the street from what had been the Stonewall Inn, now relocated a few doors away and just called Stonewall. A long line of camera-toting visitors had formed at the main entrance for their chance to photograph one another with the George Segal sculpture, Gay Liberation. *The piece depicts two gay couples, the women sitting on a park bench and the men standing nearby. It had been installed in June 1992 as a monument and memorial to the Stonewall Riots. I watched as people posed with the white bronze figures, laughing and carrying on while friends snapped photographs, and recalled the series of events that brought this monument into being, and how I came to be one of the four models for the figures in the installation.*

I FIRST met George Segal shortly after coming to New York in the spring of 1969. After a hiatus of eight years, while I was working elsewhere in the field of contemporary art, we renewed our acquaintance when I joined the staff of the Sidney Janis Gallery, which represented his work. On one of his periodic gallery visits in the spring of 1979, Segal mentioned that he had been approached by the Mildred Andrews Fund, a New Orleans-based foundation dedicated to monumental public sculpture, and a Dr. Bruce Voeller of the Mariposa Foundation. Based in New York and San Diego, Mariposa was an education, charity, and research foundation established by Voeller, who had also been a founder of the National Gay Task Force, an early and influential gay lobbying group. Together, they sought to commission Segal for a public sculpture dedicated to gay pride and the Stonewall Riots.

George asked for my opinions on the idea and I told him that I thought it could be a real challenge—and not only artistically. I had a notion that the local gay community would probably have something to say about this, as it was being planned as a permanent public statement that directly involved a groundbreaking moment in gay history, and that their concerns might pose some complications. The Mildred Andrews Fund had previously commissioned another piece from Segal, a memorial to the student killings at Kent State University. That situation had become complicated when Kent State refused the sculpture as a gift. They preferred to quietly forget what had occurred on their campus. Princeton University later accepted the work, and it was installed next to the Princeton Chapel.

Gay Liberation, *George Segal's 1992 sculpture in Christopher Park*

Several months later, Segal called me at work saying he had decided to accept the commission. He also had a favor to ask. Would I consider posing for the piece? I agreed immediately. He briefly described what he had in mind for the sculpture's configuration, and it sounded like a fine example of his typically sensitive portrayals. Once before I had posed for him, so I knew what the process entailed. But there was more to this request: would I also recruit the other three models? He wanted four "genuine homosexuals" and would leave the choices to me.

The prospect of selecting the models conjured up the premise of the old TV show *The Millionaire,* in which Michael Anthony would approach a total stranger with a check for a million dollars from a mysterious benefactor. So, rather than accost complete strangers with this unusual offer, I decided to approach people I knew who I thought would fit the bill. Eventually, after several refusals, three agreed to pose.

The New York Times had run an article by art writer and reporter Grace Glueck on July 21, 1979, officially announcing the proposal. It wasn't until the following year that the plaster version of the sculpture was to be completed, then photographed for the Janis Gallery and for submission to the various city departments for their approval, including the city's Fine Arts Commission, the Department of Parks, the Landmark's Preservation Board, and Community Board 2. This was to be Segal's first outdoor New York City sculpture, and it wasn't long before members of the gay and Village communities began to make their opinions known.

Community Board 2, the political group that represented and had jurisdiction over the neighborhood in which Christopher Park was located, held the first of three hearings on Monday evening, September 8, 1980, to present the proposal and to air the views of the residents and interested parties. In the September 11th issue of *The Westsider,* Barry Yeoman called the evening "a public hearing-*cum*-verbal bloodbath." Opinions of the proposal and sculpture ran the gamut from embittered outrage to heartfelt gratitude. Rev. Edward Hogan, Jesuit leader of the Council for Community Consciousness, stated: "My compassion is for the youngsters who will be lured into homosexuality." CUNY professor Martin Duberman was quoted as saying: "It would be nice if in our parks, human love rather than human violence could find its way," referring to the historical statuary in public parks that depict "men seated on horses, swords unsheathed, ready to charge into battle and kill."

Several gay activists spoke against the proposal, stating that the sculpture was not representative of the gay community, since the models were all "white, thirtyish, and middle class." Oscar Wilde Memorial Bookshop owner Craig Rodwell was particularly vociferous in his opposition and actively sought to prevent its installation. At the second of the three hearings, gay politician Robert Rygor called the sculpted male couple "cruising clones" and condemned Segal's figures as "grotesque stereotypes who didn't look like any gay people he chose to be friendly with."

In attendance at these hearings, and particularly miffed at Rygor's comments, I had four T-shirts printed with the words "Grotesque Stereotype" emblazoned across the front, one for each of the four models. We all attended the next hearing wearing our self-deprecating attire. When Vera Schneider, an elderly and vocal Village resident who served on three different block associations, stated her view that the sculpture was too large for the allotted space because she "knew for a fact" that the figures were larger than life-size, we models took the stage and assumed our poses, assuring her that the sculpture was no larger than the area defined by our bodies and two city park benches. Ms. Schneider insisted she knew better.

My greatest surprise was the range of vehement reactions from the gay community. Both the pro- and anti- factions circulated petitions around the Village seeking support for their opinions. The Gay Activists Alliance, an early leftist group for which Voeller himself had once served as president, issued voluminous reports on why they saw the project as negative and ill-conceived. "We do not believe that anyone should presume to commemorate the struggle for gay rights when that struggle has gone nowhere since 1969. ... We believe that legal and social equality for gay people is the only proper monument for the heroic Stonewall Rebellion." A group calling themselves Lesbians and Gay Men Against the Statue, for which Rodwell spoke at Hearing 3, distributed leaflets stating that the project was unacceptable because the entire gay community had not been consulted.

And yet, despite the disapproval expressed by these groups, an overwhelming majority of the New York gay and lesbian community liked the sculpture and wanted it installed. Segal was pressed for his reaction to the controversy, and, ever the diplomat, was quoted in James M. Saslow's account of the events as saying (in the February 1981 issue of *Christopher Street*): "The objection here seems to be that it's scandalous to express any opinion about divorce, abortion, women's rights, and homosexuals. The biggest statement I tried to make was the gentleness and humanity of homosexuals, and it shocks people to express the opinion that a homosexual is a decent, sensitive human being—and I'm shocked at that." Stated Segal in the September 22, 1980, issue of *Newsweek*: "I'm portraying gays as gentle, tender, sensitive human beings. I didn't do anything that could offend families."

GAY Liberation was first publicly shown at an exhibition at the Sidney Janis Gallery that opened on October 1, 1980, and ran through November 1. The opening night reception was a heady affair. Voeller had secured the support of dozens of national gay leaders, politicians, artists, writers, scientists, academicians, and historians, many of whom were in attendance. Bruce introduced writer Christopher Isherwood and his partner, artist Don Bachardy, who said they were honored to meet me. Though pleased by the opportunity to have helped out a friend and gallery artist, the full implications of being a model for a memorial to the Stonewall rebellion had not sunk in.

After the installation went on view, Segal received a number of bland or unfavorable reviews from art critics. In his *Christopher Street* article, Saslow, then a New York editor for *The Advocate* and an art historian at Columbia, referred to Segal as "the Edward Hopper of sculpture—the silent poet of isolation, alienation, and that peculiarly modern urban phenomenon, the lonely crowd." He went on to opine that Segal's gay couples did not seem to comply with the commission's specified theme of "positive human interaction," as there is little sign of intimacy between the two couples. "In their close-lidded inwardness, his figures seem to have withdrawn from the ruthlessly detailed tawdriness of their lives into a rigid, autistic blankness."

Michael Kimmelman, chief art critic for *The New York Times*, echoed some of these ideas in his critique of July 31, 1992, while forgiving the work for this deficiency:

> Segal's *Gay Liberation* demonstrates the traumas of creating public sculpture, particularly when the sculptures have as their subject a minority group. ... Mr. Segal's sculpture ... is in fact not stimulating or provocative or even explicit in its description of

> the relationships among the figures. As a memorial to the riots, it's deadeningly somber. Still, one feels a little sympathy for it. If public art must be art by public consensus in this divisive political climate, the work is virtually guaranteed to be without complexity and without much fascination.

Recently I asked Segal for his own reflections on the whole brouhaha, and he offered the following:

> Early on, local residents, mostly aging Italian Catholics, objected furiously to gays moving into their neighborhood, flouting their religious beliefs. I even got a letter threatening to blow up the sculpture when it was installed. Mayor Dinkins finally approved the installation. At the dedication [on June 23, 1992], amazed at the lack of religious protest, I asked a local resident, how come? He laughed and said that the older protesters had mostly died; the younger ones were indifferent. But protests starting pouring in from gays. What right did I, non-gay, have to make a sculpture on this subject? Why wasn't a black lesbian woman included in the sculpture? Why weren't all the gay groups consulted? The cacophony was shrill, and nowhere was there any mention of freedom of expression or any discussion of delicacy, restraint, regard for fellow human beings, and a long list of values important in my life.

For all the early controversy surrounding the installation and the criticism of its artistic merits, *Gay Liberation* has become an accepted institution of the West Village. It has appeared in the film version of Paul Rudnick's *Jeffrey*, as well as on the television show, *NYPD Blue*. Its familiarity and acceptance by the community makes Segal's sculpture a part of the Village landscape, a sight almost as expected as the Washington Square Arch.

More important than all the opinions from art critics and theorists, or from Greenwich Village residents and habitués, are the feelings of pride and hope that the work engenders in new generations of lesbians and gay men. They can now visit a public monument in a New York City park that memorializes and celebrates the actions of a bunch of downtrodden gay bar patrons who, one summer night, decided they had had enough abuse and rose up against a corrupt and homophobic system. We would do well to remember what they were rebelling against and how far we have come in one generation's time.

Part II

Flashback: The Roots of the Riots

The Revolution Began on the Left Coast

LILLIAN FADERMAN

THE riots that followed the 1969 raid on the Stonewall Inn in New York and the New York Gay Liberation Front that emerged from those riots were the opening salvos of a militant gay revolution. But as many of the following essays show, the struggle for gay rights had begun two decades earlier. The first gay organizations to last more than a few months, the first gay magazines, and the first gay protests were born on the other side of the continent.

Los Angeles and San Francisco could serve as crucibles for an early movement because even by the mid-20th century those cities hadn't lost entirely the effects of their "frontier town" histories.[1] In the 19th century, L.A. and San Francisco were where refugees from other parts of the United States went to be adventurous, to make their fortunes, to escape the stifling rigidities of "back home." There, on the edge of the continent, daring experimentation and action could flourish. It's not surprising, for instance, that in 1911 California became one of the first states to allow women to vote—nearly a decade before the 19th amendment extended the vote to women all over the country. By the mid-20th century, anti-homosexual laws were as draconian in California as they were elsewhere in America, but the spirit that was fostered earlier hadn't died.

In the years after World War II, the populations of L.A. and San Francisco burgeoned with gay people[2] who had been introduced to those port cities while in the military or working in the defense industry. They stayed or returned because they were drawn to the freedom the cities seemed to promise. A subterranean gay life, and soon gay organizations, flourished in both San Francisco and L.A. Dorr Legg and his African-American lover, Marvin Edwards, migrated from Detroit to L.A. in 1949, certain they could live more comfortably there than in the Midwest. A year later, Legg and another African-American man, Merton Bird, founded Knights of the Clock, a small but remarkably forward-thinking society. In an era when interracial couples were rare and taboo almost anywhere in the country—among heterosexuals and homosexuals alike—a primary purpose of Knights of the Clock, as Martha Stone points out in her essay in this section, was to help interracial gay couples find housing and jobs.

Knights of the Clock was not the only gay organization in L.A. at this time. In 1948, Harry Hay read the newly published "Kinsey Report," which said that ten percent of American men were more-or-less exclusively homosexual, and he dreamed of organizing them. That year he wrote a manifesto in which he compared the murder of homosexuals under the Nazis to the homosexual purges in the State Department, and he drew up plans for a secret organization that would fight homosexual persecution. Two years later, defining homosexuals as "an oppressed cultural minority," Hay and a handful of other men founded the Mattachine Society. As Hay recalls in his essay "Birth of a Consciousness," in 1952 Mattachine member Dale Jennings was accused by an L.A. vice squad officer of making homosexual advances. Mattachine waged an unprecedented battle. To raise money and awareness about Jennings' case, they formed the Citizens Committee to Outlaw Entrapment. And they challenged the testimony of the police in court. Mattachine's legal victory astonished even gay people, who were not used to winning against the police. New chapters cropped up in San Francisco, New York, Chicago, and Washington, D.C.

The country's first lesbian organization, Daughters of Bilitis (DOB), was also born on the Left Coast. As Del Martin and Phyllis Lyon recount in "Lesbian Liberation Begins," their organization, which started in San Francisco in 1955, was founded as a safe alternative to lesbian bars, where raids were always a threat. Though DOB's social function remained its primary appeal for many members, the organization's leaders nudged them toward political action. For instance, Del Martin declared in the December 1956 issue of *The Ladder*, DOB's new, nationally circulated magazine, that homosexuals "are citizens of the United States, and as such are entitled to those civil rights set forth in the Constitution," and she suggested as early as 1960 that a unified homosexual vote could influence elections. "We do have a voice in the affairs of the community and the nation," she exhorted DOB members in *The Ladder*. "Let's make it a strong one."

The same year that *The Ladder* began publishing, Mattachine headquarters moved to San Francisco and also started a nationally circulated magazine, *Mattachine Review*, which served a vital purpose in disseminating information that most gay people could find nowhere else. Its first issue, for instance, included an account by UCLA psychologist Dr. Evelyn Hooker about her L.A.-based study which demonstrated that, on major psychological tests such as the Rorschach, healthy male homosexuals could not be distinguished from healthy male heterosexuals. Therefore, "homosexuality" could not legitimately be considered a diagnostic category. (Two decades later her study would help convince the American Psychiatric Association to declassify "homosexuality" from its *Diagnostic and Statistical Manual of Mental Disorders*).[3]

But *The Ladder* and *Mattachine Review* were not the first gay or lesbian publications in America. The first was a low-circulation lesbian magazine, *Vice Versa*, published in L.A. from June 1947 to February 1948, which featured vehement proclamations such as (in the September 1947 issue) "The Third Sex is here to stay!" and fierce excoriations (in June 1947) of "self-styled judges who smugly carve the standards for society." The second gay publication in America, *ONE*, was started by members of Los Angeles Mattachine in 1952. Two years later, when the office of the L.A. postmaster declared that *ONE* magazine could not be mailed because it contained material that was "obscene, lewd, lascivious, and filthy," *ONE* hired a lawyer who took the case all the way to the U.S. Supreme Court. In 1958, the Court concluded that *ONE* was indeed a homosexual magazine as the postmaster had complained, but that did not mean the publication was obscene. The Post Office had no right to confiscate *ONE*, the Supreme Court declared. This was the first national gay victory in U.S. history.

As forward-looking as those mid-20th-century periodicals were, their readership was minuscule compared to that of *The Advocate*, which started in L.A. as a newsletter after a brutal raid on January 1, 1967, of an L.A. gay bar, the Black Cat, discussed in this section by Eve Goldberg. *The Advocate,* which became a newspaper and then a magazine, moved to the San Francisco Bay Area in 1974 and later returned to L.A. (Its present circulation of 175,000 makes it America's most-read LGBT magazine.)

California also saw some of the first gay protests in America. John Rechy remembers in "*Lawrence* Brought It All Back Home" that more than a decade before Stonewall, he was in a gay mini-riot against harassing police in downtown L.A. San Francisco saw another mini-riot in 1966, when about fifty black and Latino "queens" fought police harassment in their favorite hangout, Compton's Cafeteria.[4] Californians also made their anger over anti-gay injustices felt in ways short of rioting. In 1951, when authorities tried to suspend the liquor license of San Francisco's Black Cat Café because it catered to homosexuals, its owner, Sol Stoumen, took the case to the California Supreme Court. The Court restored Stoumen's liquor license, finding that even homosexuals had the right to free association.[5] The 1967 raid on L.A.'s Black Cat was answered by a peaceful public protest that drew 500 demonstrators. The following year saw a dramatic "flower power" protest by gays wielding armfuls of bouquets and occupying the Harbor Division Police Station after a raid on The Patch, a Southern California gay bar. "We're Americans, too!" the protestors had screamed at the raiding police.[6] By spring 1969, some gay activists in California were eschewing flower power in favor of images influenced by Black Power. For instance, with more than a passing nod to the Black Panthers, a gay group that staged angry pickets of anti-gay businesses in San Francisco and L.A. dubbed itself "the Pink Panthers."[7]

Lesbians and gays on the Left Coast were not the only ones, of course, to protest and agitate for change in the years before Stonewall. John D'Emilio points out in "Frank Kameny Takes It Public" that Kameny, in Washington, D.C., pressed the movement in a more militant and assertive direction than it had ever had, beginning with the 1965 picketing he led in front of the White House, the State Department, and the Pentagon.

But courageous as all these protests of the 1950s and '60s were, none was "the hairpin drop heard round the world," as New York Mattachine president Dick Leitsch immediately recognized the Stonewall Riots to be in the July 1969 issue of his organization's newsletter. What accounts for the spontaneous explosion of

Stonewall was less the preceding twenty years of gay organizing and protest than the widespread militancy and turbulence that characterized the 1960s in big cities throughout America: from the Black Power movement, to the long succession of summertime Black riots, to the huge antiwar movement with its sometimes violent demonstrations, to the riots at the 1968 Democratic Convention in Chicago. In the hot summer of the following year, all of that together led to Stonewall.

October 2018

FOOTNOTES

1. The effects of San Francisco's and Los Angeles' frontier histories on later gay communities are discussed in Nan Alamilla Boyd's *Wide-Open Town: A History of Queer San Francisco to 1965* (University of California Press, 2003); and Lillian Faderman and Stuart Timmons in *Gay L.A.: A History of Sexual Outlaws, Power Politics, and Lipstick Lesbians* (Basic Books, 2006).
2. In the mid-20th century "gay" was an umbrella term that described people who would be called "LGBT" in the 21st century.
3. I discuss Evelyn Hooker's study and the APA's declassification of homosexuality in *The Gay Revolution: The Story of the Struggle* (Simon and Schuster, 2015).
4. *Screaming Queens: The Riot at Compton's Cafeteria,* a documentary by Susan Stryker and Victor Silverman, 2005.
5. *Sol Stoumen v. George R. Reilly,* 37 Cal., 2d 713, S.F. no. 18310, August 28, 1951.
6. "Patch Fights Three-Way Battle," *Los Angeles Advocate,* August 1968; and Dick Michaels, "Patch Raids Police Station," *Los Angeles Advocate,* September 1968.
7. "Homo Revolt Blasting Off on Two Fronts," *Berkeley Barb,* April 11-17, 1969; Leo E. Laurence, "Gay Revolution," *Vector,* April 1969; and Leo E. Laurence, "Gay Strike Hits Southern California, *Berkeley Barb,* May 2-8, 1970.

Harry Hay, *by Charles Hefling*

Birth of a Consciousness

HARRY HAY

THERE are, I imagine, a number of people who wonder, not necessarily what woodwork American 20th-century queers materialized out of, but where did the gay movement come from?

In the 1930s and '40s, there were clusters of homosexuals all over the country impassioned to get a group of some sort going. Two or three brothers would meet for supper and spark up a storm of ideas. By the second meeting, word would get out that such doings were a novel way to cruise, and by the third meeting attendance would double. But when the fourth meeting didn't produce any more new faces, the fifth would get only the by-now burned-out Sparkers of the first. Fini! There wouldn't be a sixth meeting. And this pattern would repeat itself over and over, year after year.

What was the social climate in which all this would be occurring? In the 1920s and '30s, single men didn't, as a general rule, earn enough to live in apartments. They lived in boarding houses. The word "homosexual," a technical adjective in the penal code characterizing illegal aberrations in heterosexual behavior, did not yet appear in any standard dictionary. "Homosexual," as a technical adjective, designated heterosexual men who occasionally were apprehended for engaging in perverted or degenerate acts. These monstrous practices, denounced by biblical and traditional common laws alike, were considered not only social but also political crimes against community standards, crimes that had to be obliterated whenever detected. People who had fallen so low as to engage in them must either be cured for their own good, forcibly if necessary, or be put away for the protection of society.

This general attitude, maintained by both Church and State, vigorously expounded on the front pages of the press and periodically denounced by the editorial sections, guaranteed that the established limits of decorum were being observed by the community. Nineteenth-century America, however else it might have perceived itself, was socially divided into two groups, those who kept up with the Joneses and considered themselves respectable—and then there were those others! Borrowing from the French author Alexandre Dumas, those others were the demimondaine, the shadowy half-world people who chose not to show themselves by the full light of day but only in the twilight. Actors, opera singers, ballet dancers, vaudeville performers, professional card-sharps, riverboat gamblers, acrobats, jugglers, musclemen, magicians, clairvoyants, soothsayers—the women you would never bring home to meet your mother, the men you would never let your sister marry.

From the point of view of the people of the demimonde, the twilight world made perfect sense. It was their world, and its traditional and particular multicultural morality suited their lifestyle. Touring circuses, theater companies, or vaudeville acts straggling from town to town were never welcome except in designated disreputable hotels and boarding houses, and even here they were permitted to enter only by the servants' entrance. Such was "the gay world" in the 19th century, and this pattern did not change, even in the U.S., until the demise of vaudeville [in the 1930s]. The gay twilight world was made for those who slept by day and rose in the afternoon, those who took afternoon coffee and a croissant at kiosks along the street, along riverbanks, or in parks. This gathering of shadows in the waning light was for those who took brisk turns along winding paths as afternoons turned to twilight and lamps began to bloom between trees in early evening. This twilit world was for those who met one another along these walks and shared biscuits and wine before repairing to whatever stage or music hall they might be engaged with.

The downside of the twilight world was that, because its milieus were necessarily places of shadow and darkness where thieves and thugs and blackmailers also abounded, it was a world outside of the law. The people who frequented this world did so at their own risk, and when, as happened quite frequently, there was a police roundup of scoundrels and malefactors in such areas—usually not carried out until after the entertainers had gone off to their several billets—and innocent or unsuspecting bystanders were inadvertently caught up in such a sweep, they stood to lose not only their reputations, but also, when the story was published with pictures on the front page of the newspaper, their lodgings and livelihoods as well. When the police sweeps related to immoral behavior, the social and political ostracism was immediate and total. Homosexual behavior was a despised heterosexual perversion according to law, medicine, and religion. If a person was discovered harboring homosexual inclinations, he was adjudged a heterosexual who had gone bad, who had become degenerate—someone not to be tolerated in decent society.

WHEN I was growing up in the 1920s, and was grown in the 1930s, this was what we all heard night and day, day in and day out; it was in the air you breathed. There were those who, like me, didn't believe it, who knew that what we carried was a shining, golden, pulsating dream, a wonderful alternative window to goodness, for which as yet we had no words—and somehow I knew that I was going to find some words for it. There were those who felt they couldn't help being what they were, and who formed little cliques when they were lucky enough to find others like themselves. But there were those who never found another of these "twilight men." And there were those who hated being what they were, those who tried to drown their self-loathing in liquor or drugs, and who cruised dangerously.

Our greatest dangers in such outlaw decades were from sneak-raids on public cruising places—always in the three-month stretch just before an election—ABC raids (for Alcoholic Beverage Commission) on those few bars that occasionally would serve you drinks in a dark corner at four times the going price. From 1935 on, blackmailers and the vice squad had nightly quotas of entrapments to carry out. Of all these dangers, the gravest threat to the twilight world—from the 1830s through the 1970s—at all times was public exposure and censure. Arrest in a raid, publication of your name in the paper, automatically guaranteed that you would be seen as guilty even before the trial. The cops would call your boss, so you usually lost your job; they would call your landlord, so you'd lose your lodging. The insurance companies would cancel your policies if you had a car. Entrapment usually guaranteed exposure unless your lawyer was able to fix it so you could cop to a lesser charge by bribing the arresting detective or softening up the judge. Otherwise, it would be a felony sentence of up to six or ten years in a state prison on a first offense. After you had completed your sentence on a first conviction, you would be required to register with the police every time you moved, for the rest of your life. A second conviction—in any category of a "morals" charge—and you would be sent to Atascadero State Prison to be cured of your depravity. Atascadero gave you a choice of "curing" method: castration or lobotomy. These conditions ruled our lives and loves in the state of California until State Penal Code item #541-C-C was amended by rescinding portions of its subsections in 1975.

It's an old but still useful cliché among progressives and trade union activists that, socially or politically, the middle class has never produced anything of significance, because middle-class people, regardless of how collectively motivated they may be, always have personal investments to protect—a career they have worked years to develop, a social or political position they have sacrificed so much to attain. Any political movement would have to originate from below. My first Mattachine Society was no exception. It emerged equally from the rough-and-tumble trade-union organizing experiences of one of us [four founders] and from the outlaw underground community organizing experiences undertaken in the previous decade by the other three. We all knew how to invoke the U.S. Constitution's Fifth Amendment to protect membership lists or activities from unwelcome scrutiny, if and when the local police or the Feds got nosey. Like experienced left-wing fellow travelers everywhere, we all automatically assumed we would be infiltrated by the FBI. And, as it turned out, we were not wrong.

For us queers, the political climate at the state and local levels had been ominous forever: social behavior and morality had always been matters of states' and municipalities' concern. But our federal rights, our labor-union rights to organize and develop social programs, had never been questioned. Now suddenly, in 1948, the political climate had turned ominous. Senator Joseph McCarthy's scurrilous House Un-American Activities Committee (HUAC) witch hunt, the disgracing of Hollywood actors, writers, and directors who were Marxist-oriented activists or sympathizers, had dragged on for months, terrifying decent people into becoming public snitches. All this demoralized the nation's entire cultural environment. "Loyalty oaths" became ubiquitous, a prerequisite for public or professional employment. America seemed to be moving rapidly toward the type of police state in which public scapegoating had already proven itself to be a highly effective and inexpensive form of control. With President Truman's rush to recognize the new state of Israel, with his push to integrate Negroes into the armed forces, with the further integration of blacks into organized labor, it was obvious to me, as I wrote in the original Call-to-Organize in 1948, that the political scapegoat victim this time around would be us, the queers! We had to begin finding out who we were, what we might be able to be for: we had to organize!

EVEN with copies of my "Call-to-Organize" and a new book, Alfred Kinsey's 1948 *Sexual Behavior in the Human Male* (which I carried to give me credibility), it took me two long, lonely, scary years to find my first recruit [Rudi Gernreich, who was also Hay's lover]. Forming a society of two, and determined to get a discussion group going, we went to an unmarked section of Santa Monica Beach that we knew was frequented by gay brothers. Because the media were whipping up support for the Korean War and Red Scare hysteria was going full blast, we figured that asking brothers to sign our Stockholm Peace Petition would be so radical that they'd be more interested in agreeing to come to a "Kinsey Report" discussion group, right? Wrong! By the end of the summer, we had gotten 500 signatures on our petition, and had found not one person who would dare come to our discussion group, so overpowering was the terror of police reprisal or blackmail.

The next three members [Bob Hull, Dale Jennings, and Chuck Rowland] came out of the 1950 fall historical materialism music classes that I had developed for teaching people's songs at the Southern California Labor School. We—the first five of the group that we would call the Mattachine Society five months later—all had previously trained in underground struggles for social and political justice. We knew that we brothers were of a different consciousness from the heterosexuals around us. We knew we were not the degraded, degenerate monsters that society's laws and religious prejudices made us out to be. But we also knew that we didn't yet have the concepts, let alone the words, to say so.

At our first discussion group, in December 1950, eighteen of us sat for two hours not really knowing what to say to one another but sensing that no one wanted to leave. At the second meeting, to break the ice, the three of us present from the five-member steering committee started the ball rolling by "coming out" to one another. After about two hours of this, it suddenly flashed on us all that just maybe we each had more in common with the others in this room, friends and newcomers alike, than we had ever had with anybody before, in all our lives! For the first time in any of our experience, we were feeling the prickling surge of collective Brotherhood.

The core group realized that by this process we'd turned a major corner in our perception of gay consciousness. People couldn't wait for the next meeting to learn more about each other, and so about themselves through the experiences of others, and to bring a friend. The golden dream of Brotherhood was enveloping us all. Twenty years later, in the 1970s, this process would be known as "consciousness-raising raps." But in 1951, we had not developed such concepts, let alone the words. We just knew we had invented the organizing tool we'd been looking for. This contagious fever for brotherhood developed for the First Mattachine a mailing list of about 5,000 people in California alone, in 1952, right in the teeth of Senator McCarthy's witch hunt!

Of course, our luck didn't last: our very excitement attracted the first wave of opportunistic, middle-class assimilationists, the negative-imaging homosexuals so unlike the joyous, positive-imaging gay brotherhood of the earlier pioneering wave—opportunists who would insist that we were all exactly the same as heterosexuals except in bed, and that we had nothing in common with one another except our sexual inclinations. My first Mattachine Society set itself the task of functioning by unanimity. Over the next two and half years, 27 Brotherhood Guilds were established. Each guild was responsible for two discussion groups a month. Discussion groups could range from less than fifteen at one meeting to more than 75 at the next. In the course of the first blooming, the Society undertook to publicize and openly defend a vice squad entrapment case against one of its members [Dale Jennings], forcing the city of Los Angeles to withdraw the charges, in the summer of 1952.

This victory brought on that wave of opportunists, expropriating everything in the way of their own assimilationist agenda—thus trampling the bloom of the guild brotherhoods in the process. Still, the sudden burst of marvelous fairy inventiveness involved in publicizing this campaign and raising funds for it was unprecedented.

The Lester Horton Dance Theater hosted perhaps the first theater performance benefit for gay concerns in our history and drew a full house. A weekend dance and beach party at Zuma Beach attracted over 500 paying guests during its sixty hours of revelry; and we papered certain areas of the city, including bus stops, with upwards of 10,000 pieces of literature on three occasions.

Out of the heady swirls of cultural togetherness that these five months of activity engendered, a dozen or so Mattachiners coalesced to start the first ongoing gay magazine in the U.S., *One, the Homosexual Viewpoint*, which first appeared in January 1953 and continued to appear monthly for nearly twenty years. ONE Inc., which in 1955 had been barred by the U.S. Post Office from distributing sexually-oriented materials through the mails, sued and won a Supreme Court decision in 1958 to the effect that gay-oriented materials may be sent through the mails provided they contained material of artistic and/or educational merit. *One*, recognizing the clarion call of its masthead, Thomas Carlyle's lovely phrase, "A mystic bond of brotherhood makes all men one," launched the first nationwide annual Homophile Cultural Conference in January of 1954.

The second wave of Mattachine Societies—the hetero-imitative "Robert's Rules of Order" opportunists who had nothing in common with each other but their sexual inclination—were mainly concerned about getting their several states' laws changed, a quest they soon discovered they had neither the organization nor the experience to accomplish. Business-like, no-nonsense chapters met in L.A. and San Francisco in the fall of 1953 and the spring of 1954. By the fall of 1954, the L.A. chapter had gotten bored and started to decline, but San Francisco had started *The Mattachine Review* in the summer of 1954, and its success would keep a semblance of a chapter alive for three or four years.

In 1955 two lesbian couples in San Francisco would found the Daughters of Bilitis with its own publication, *The Ladder*, which would also continue to appear for nearly twenty years. Like the second wave of the Mattachine Society, the DOB would spread several chapters across the country, likewise middle-class, orderly, and respectable, although probably never as hypocritically respectable as was the Denver Mattachine under the leadership, in 1956, of the Rev. Carl Harding, who recommended that all homosexual men marry heterosexually and keep a boy on the side.

In 1957, '58, and '59, the Denver, San Francisco, and New York Mattachine chapters mounted a National Mattachine Convention in one of the three cities. It was mostly for show, but the events did develop the outlines of inter-city and inter-state relations. In San Francisco, in 1959, a representative from the mayor's office was introduced to the Assembly, and his remarks attracted the brief attention of the local press. Fliers were being circulated; word was getting around; homophiles as political entities were beginning to emerge. Homophiles disguised as hetero-imitative assimilationists were noted for being present on occasion, although their opinions were not yet being sought.

But the golden dream of brotherhood, which had bloomed so buoyantly in the first Mattachine Guilds, had been snuffed out, not to appear again until we once more started using a variation of the "coming-out-to-one-another" process at an encounter-type community outreach conference in San Francisco in May 1969. And that had set us back for years! The middle-class assimilationists who inundated us first in the fall of 1952 wasted First Mattachine's golden dream of brotherhood and totally scotched the notion that we might be a cultural minority. Yet when Stonewall burst onto the scene sixteen years later, the new brothers and sisters assumed everybody had always known we were a cultural minority since Day One!

The Radicalism of Harry Hay

WILL ROSCOE

ON August 10, 1948, Harry Hay wrote a prospectus that anticipated the goals, forms, and institutions of today's international lesbian, gay, bisexual, and transgender movement to an extent that was truly prophetic. For the next six decades, he brooded over this new movement as it sputtered to life, nudging it onto its feet in the 1950s, steeling its resolve in the 1960s, challenging it to claim its rightful place among the great causes of our time, until 2002, when, still grumbling and grousing, still issuing alarums and calls, his brow furrowed at the horizon, he passed away. He was ninety.

I want first to acknowledge the importance of Harry Hay—his activism and ideas, and his remarkable body of work. It's a radical enterprise—in the sense of the word that Hay liked to point out, "to the root." For in exploring Hay's life and thought we will be returning to the roots of LGBT liberation, contemplating not only its proximate causes and circumstances, but also the nature of the inner conflict that finds its resolution in an act of sheer audacity: declaring an identity, signing up for a cause. And if you have difficulty putting together the idea of "major historical figure" and "really big queen"—well, you've come to the right place! Because I will argue that this drama queen, in his Holy Fool outfit of jeans and camouflage skirt and fake pearls, ranks among the most inspiring and courageous civil rights leaders in American history.

In the 1950s, Hay was not alone, nor was he the first to challenge society's treatment of homosexuals. Writers like Robert Duncan, Gore Vidal, and James Baldwin all published works offering a defense of homosexuals and challenging the prejudice against us. Social scientists like Alfred Kinsey, Donald Webster Cory, and Evelyn Hooker were taking on the biases of their disciplines. And activists like Paul Goodman, Bayard Rustin, and David McReynolds were beginning to step out of the closet. But Harry Hay did something none of these others did: he called a meeting.

Hay is best known for his role in starting up the original Mattachine Society in Los Angeles. Between 1950 and 1953, Harry Hay, Chuck Rowland, Dale Jennings, Bob Hull, Konrad Stevens, James Gruber, and Rudi Gernreich built an organization that used consciousness-raising groups to recruit members; held fundraisers, events, and lectures; spun off a publication; successfully defended one of its members against entrapment; distributed flyers and leaflets; and began polling political candidates. By 1953, perhaps 5,000 people in northern and southern California had attended Mattachine activities.

Then, when a local newspaper columnist hinted darkly that a "strange new pressure group" named Mattachine might include communists, some members panicked. Hay, of course, was a big commie, as were some of the other organizers. Two conventions were called in the spring of 1953. On vote after vote, the founders and their original vision were affirmed. But red-baiting by conservative dissidents and the fear of investigation led the founders to make a dramatic decision. To give the organization a clean slate, they all resigned.

Make no mistake: the founders were not booted out or voted down. The grassroots, activist Mattachine was betrayed by assimilationists who were threatening to take names to the FBI. But even more heartbreaking, the story of early Mattachine was suppressed. The young activists of the post-Stonewall years—my generation—had no idea that a grassroots, liberation-based movement had existed before. Not until Jonathan Ned Katz' 1976 *Gay American History* did we know, and what a surprise it was, that an activist movement had flourished over a quarter of a century earlier. And it had all been thought up by a man who used theory and skills he had learned as a card-carrying member of the Communist Party. What's more, he was still alive!

And who would have predicted that Hay would return to L.A. in 1979 and resume a life of renewed activism, and along the way help launch yet another movement—the unruly, indefinable, incomparable Radical Faeries? Then, in 1990, we got Stuart Timmons' masterful biography, *The Trouble with Harry Hay*, its pages brimming with the names of the activists, actors, artists, writers, musicians, dancers, political figures, and others whom Hay had known, a who's who of bohemian Los Angeles in the mid-20th century. And Hay continued to make high-profile interventions into GLBT politics well into his seventies and eighties, whenever he felt voices were being excluded. But his greatest contribution was the breakthrough that enabled him to see queer folks as a people.

IT is almost impossible for us to imagine the consciousness of a time when there simply was no such group. As Hay so often pointed out to anyone who would listen, when he was a young man there was no word for talking about "us"—no common term that didn't amount to a malediction or provoke nervous giggles. We were "that way," "sensitive," or "touched"; "aunties," "nan cies," or "fairies." Nothing frustrated Hay more than the anachronistic projection of our modern self-awareness onto the times he lived in as a young man. Hay's point was that the leap from adjective to noun had not been made, and until it had, sexual minorities did not and could not think about themselves in collective ways. It was literally unthinkable.

In the 1930s, when Hay suggested to his boyfriend, Will Geer—the leftist actor who ended his career playing Grandpa Walton—that they start a society of "us" and have serious discussions, Geer snapped back: "But honey, what would we talk about?"

Geer was putting it politely. Henry Gerber, a leftist activist like Hay, who also tried to "call a meeting" in Chicago in the 1920s, provides a blunter appraisal of the prospects Hay faced. "The first difficulty," Gerber recalled, "was in rounding up enough members and contributors so the work could go forward. The average homosexual, I found, was ignorant concerning himself. Others were fearful. Still others were frantic or depraved. Some were blasé. Many homosexuals told me that their search for forbidden fruit was the real spice of life. With this argument they rejected our aims. We wondered how we could accomplish anything with such resistance from our own people."

So how do you call a political meeting of a group of people who call each other the "friends of Dorothy"? Will Geer's question was the Gordian Knot that had to be cut if there was to be a movement. For Hay, the answer came in 1948. That August he attended a party of what turned out to be all gay men. He had a copy of "the Kinsey Report" under his arm, and he had just come from signing a petition to place Henry Wallace's name on the California ballot as a candidate for president. Beer flowed, talk followed, and that night a new idea was born.

Wallace's third-party candidacy was drawing support from many activists like Hay, whose roots lay in the Popular Front politics of the 1930s and '40s. This was the period when American Communists forged alliances with a wide range of groups that opposed fascism and the worst ills of capitalism. In America, opposing fascism meant fighting racism. The party lent aid to African-American causes and organizations, and wide-ranging discussions among party intellectuals extended Marxist principles to make the case that cultural, racial, and ethnic minorities had common cause with the working class—over and against an older view that considered minorities the byproduct of capitalism's attempt to divide and conquer.

In Southern California, not uniquely but especially, African-Americans were one of several groups experiencing racism, and they all had a common enemy in brutally repressive law enforcement agencies and local governments dominated by business interests. The communists worked with them all. And so, in mid-20th century, as Daniel Hurewitz shows in *Bohemian Los Angeles* (2007), we see the chrysalis of what was to come—multiculturalism, an analysis of the relationship between class and both racism and sexism, and the ever-shifting coalitional politics that are now so characteristic of the American city.

Meanwhile, at the 1948 party in an apartment in L.A., the discussion ranged from Kinsey and his startling revelations regarding homosexuality to the Wallace campaign. Hay tossed out the idea that a discreet organization, calling itself perhaps, Bachelors for Wallace, could lobby for a plank supporting the right to privacy. The idea took off. At dawn's early light, the revelers straggled home to sleep it off. But not Hay, who was pouring coffee and sitting down at the typewriter.

When he pulled out the last sheet of paper, he had created a prospectus of brazen scope. In this text he used the capitalized word "Minority" fourteen times in the phrase "Androgynous Minority," but that adjective was soon replaced with "homophile," then later still with "gay," "faerie," and "third gender," among others. But the noun was always "minority"—and this was new. The other Mattachine organizers challenged Hay to flesh out this idea.

Chuck Rowland recalled, "I kept saying, 'What is our theory?' Having been a Communist, you've got to work with a theory. 'What is our basic principle that we are building on?' And Hay said, 'We are an oppressed cultural minority.' And I said, 'That's exactly it!'"

Hay's ideas were discussed extensively by the founders at discussion groups and in presentations by Hay. When the group adopted a mission statement in 1951, it referred to homosexuals as an "oppressed minority." The organizers put the theory to practice. The thesis states that we are a group, so discussions were centered around the questions this idea generated: What do we all have common? What experiences do we share? How can we help each other? The results were powerfully cathartic—and by 1953 the discussion groups had proliferated.

The most fully developed version of the thesis exists in notes that Hay wrote in 1960. He began by borrowing the definition of cultural minorities from a text he used in his Marxist classes, one often cited in the party's discussions about African-Americans, which states: "A nation [that here has the sense of "a people," or a minority, within a larger state] is a historically-evolved, stable community of language, territory, economic life and psychological make-up manifested in a community of culture." No single characteristic is determinative, "only a sum total of characteristics, of which, when nations are compared, one characteristic (national character), or another (language), or a third (territory, economic conditions), stands out in sharper relief." As Hay sums it up, all groups "whose motivating persuasions and/or fundamental inclinations evoke decisive patterns towards a socially specific way of life, are to be seen as Social Minorities."

Hay provided several examples to show the variety of ways in which minority identities could be constituted and then creatively reformulated to survive over time. Two were especially key to his argument. The Nisei were the Japanese-Americans interned during World War II, a racist policy that Communists like Hay had protested. Had the Nisei been deported to Japan, as was threatened, their American outlook would have marked them as a minority there as well, even though they remained racially and linguistically Japanese. Similarly, the former American slaves who established a colony in Liberia were black but no longer African; they became a minority within the nation they created.

In each case, social and historical contingencies trumped essential traits. Now Hay turned to the case of modern homosexuals. They do not come from a single race or have a single language; they do not have cross-generational kinship systems. But Hay argued that they have two of the four variables in his paradigm: a shared psychological make-up or outlook and distinctive modes of communication. In light of his previous examples, this is enough. As for the other variables, Hay noted, they can be "historically constituted."

I call this the "cultural minority lite" thesis or the existential version. It says that common experiences of being queer, of facing hostile families and communities, learning strategies for surviving, finding others like us, and the values that accrue from these experiences, provide sufficient common bonds for a movement and the seeds of a culture. This version does not make transcendental claims regarding a continuous past or essential traits. It cannot be accused of essentialism in the way that Hay is usually labeled. But as Hay's thinking developed, he elaborated this thesis into what I call the full-on or "transcendental" version of the cultural minority theory. Although more controversial and easily stereotyped, I think it is a richer, more provocative hypothesis than the existential version, and it is equally grounded in Marxist thinking.

Already by 1960, Hay's research had convinced him that "we" had a place in history that transcended modernity. And here is where the two exemplars he cited so often were key—the so-called two-spirit or berdache role of Native North America (which has many parallels worldwide) and the Fool, a folkloric figure in Renaissance Europe that Hay believed was a survival of an ancient, pre-Christian, agrarian village role. Hay concluded that these roles were based on craft and religious specialization. Crafts being tied to production, religion to the redistribution of surpluses, this means that roles such as these are not epiphenomena of the superstructure but integral to the social relations of production, the central subject of Marxism.

SINCE Stonewall, the existential model of GLBT identity has been enough to unite us. It has given us an effective civil rights moment, a lively culture of resistance, and bonds of amazing strength that sustained us through the AIDS epidemic. But Hay believed that GLBT people had a deep yearning to see themselves as having a more meaningful place in the human story. A doubt remains at the core: If I'm not sick or deviant, if I'm normal, why don't I have a history? And if I'm different, what's the purpose of it? Hay's thinking encompasses either and both of these models: the minority lite version, grounded in the existential experience of being queer in America; and the full-on transcendental version, grounding us in the broadest narratives of human history. Both affirm identity, both affirm progressive identity politics.

This piece was adapted from a keynote speech by the author titled "Radical Love, Visionary Politics: The Adventure of Harry Hay," which was delivered at a conference called "Radically Gay: The Life and Visionary Legacy of Harry Hay," held September 27–30, 2012, in New York City.

Lesbian Liberation Begins

DEL MARTIN AND PHYLLIS LYON

WE ARE erroneously given credit as the founders of the Daughters of Bilitis in San Francisco in 1955. It wasn't even our idea. A young Filipina immigrant envisioned a club for lesbians here in the States that would give us an opportunity to meet and socialize (and especially to dance) outside of the gay bars that were frequently raided by police. Meeting in each others' homes provided us with privacy and a sense of safety from the police and gawking tourists in the bars. Personally, our motivation was simply to meet other lesbians. There were eight of us in the beginning: four couples, four blue-collar and four white-collar workers, two lesbian mothers, and two women of color.

This new secret club, which would later become the first national lesbian organization, was named the Daughters of Bilitis to sound like just another women's lodge. Bilitis (pronounced Bil-E-tis) came from *The Songs of Bilitis* by Pierre Louÿs, a long narrative love poem in which Bilitis was cast as a contemporary of Sappho on the Isle of Lesbos. Presumably lesbians would know what the name meant. If anyone else asked, we could say we belonged to a Greek poetry club. In 1958, when renting our first office suite on O'Farrell Street across from Macy's, Del told the building manager that DOB was "an organization concerned with the sociological problems of single women."

The Daughters began in a climate of fear, rejection, and oppression, the aftermath of Congressional hearings and witch hunts by Wisconsin Senator Joseph McCarthy, who was relentless in "exposing" Communists and homosexuals in government. Lesbians and gay men, if found out, were subject to reprisals from all quarters of society: employers, police, military, government, family, and friends. After bar raids, police often informed employers or gave lists of arrestees to the newspapers. Parents disowned their adult children. Minors were sent to a shrink or were institutionalized and given shock (or other) treatments. Purges occurred periodically on military bases. Just having "tendencies" or being friends with lesbians could get you a court martial and a dishonorable discharge. Many people lost licenses and their professional careers. Lesbian mothers were denied custody of their children and even visitation rights in some cases. The law, religion, and psychiatry all played a role in the cruel treatment of lesbians and gay men by society and family. There was no sense of community as exists today. Lesbians were isolated and separated—and scared.

By 1956, we found that there were two other organizations: the Mattachine Society in San Francisco and ONE, Inc. in Los Angeles. They welcomed DOB into the "homophile" movement, but chided us for being separatists. Both Mattachine and ONE were open to both sexes but were overwhelmingly male in membership and program. They were glad to see women getting involved.

Plagued by people's fear of having their names on mailing or membership lists, DOB was constantly hampered in its outreach. Along with parties and discussion groups, the early days involved

Del Martin and Phyllis Lyon, by Charles Hefling

a great deal of peer counseling to help overcome the stigma of being branded illegal, immoral, and sick by a hostile society. After its first year, DOB had only fifteen members, although more attended parties and discussions. The group started publishing *The Ladder* and conducting public forums in a downtown auditorium.

The "1st Rung" of *The Ladder* was published by the Daughters "from the city of many moods," San Francisco, in October 1956, with Phyllis as editor. It included the four-fold purpose of DOB: 1) education of the variant to enable her to understand herself and make her adjustment to society; 2) education of the public to break down erroneous conceptions, taboos, and prejudices; 3) participation in research projects to further knowledge about the homosexual; 4) investigation of the penal code and promotion of changes through state legislatures.

The second issue focused on convincing what few readers *The Ladder* had that "Your name is safe!" An editorial cited the 1953 decision of the Supreme Court (*U.S. v. Rumely*) upholding the right of a publisher to refuse to reveal the names of purchasers of reading material to a Congressional investigating committee. That issue was mailed to every woman attorney listed in the telephone directory. The response was overwhelming: "Take me off your mailing list or I will report you to the postal authorities."

There was one positive response from Attorney Juliet Lowenthal. She and her attorney husband Morris had fought the Black Cat bar case (*Stoumen v. Reilly*) all the way to the California Supreme Court to determine that homosexuals had the right to congregate in public places. Later, when the Lowenthals submitted an amicus brief in the case against Mary's First and Last Chance lesbian bar in Oakland (*Vallerga v. Munro*), they cited and filed the September and October 1958 issues of *The Ladder* with the District Court of Appeals. The "misconduct" in the state's case against the bar owners consisted of women dressed in masculine attire, a "female with her arms round another female, kissing themselves on the cheeks and necks, and a waitress calling an undercover policewoman a 'cute little bitch.'" The case went all the way to the State Supreme Court, which found that this conduct was not "inimical to the public welfare or morals," but merely an indication that the clientele was homosexual. The Court also observed that homosexuals should not be expected to exhibit a higher standard of conduct than that expected of other (heterosexual) citizens.

FROM the beginning, DOB was engaged in peer counseling and internal discussion groups to allay fears and build self-esteem. Holding public forums allowed lesbians and some gay and transgendered men to attend without committing themselves. Professional speakers included attorneys who explained the law and told us what our rights were and what to do in case of arrest. Those in the mental health professions refuted the sickness theory and promoted self-acceptance. Our contention was that once you accepted yourself, regardless of what others had to say, you could cope better in a hostile society. The professionals who were among society's decision makers gave us the validation we needed then.

In February 1957, the Daughters of Bilitis proudly announced that it had become a full-fledged nonprofit corporation under the laws of the state of California. "It was a signal of our legality and our permanency as an organization," reported *The Ladder*.

As representatives of DOB, we attended the 1959 Mattachine convention in Denver, where Del appeared on a panel and expressed her annoyance at always having to defend DOB as a separate and distinct women's organization. She pointed out that both coed groups assumed that whatever was said about homosexuality included lesbians, just like the generic term "he." Del said: "Lesbians are not satisfied to be auxiliary members or second-class homosexuals. ... One of Mattachine's aims is that of sexual equality. May I suggest that you start with the lesbian? This would certainly be a 'new frontier in acceptance of the homophile' [the theme of the convention]."

This was also the convention at which a new member, William Brandhove, hoodwinked the Mattachine Society into passing a resolution praising San Francisco Mayor George Christopher and Police Chief Thomas Cahill for an enlightened administration in "sociological problem areas." Brandhove claimed the resolution had been mailed to him by members of the S.F.P.D., who requested its passage. We knew there was something wrong and reminded Mattachine members that this was an election year and asked what earthly use it would be to Christopher to gain the endorsement of the Mattachine Society? It wasn't. Brandhove was a plant for Christopher's opponent, Assessor Russ Wolden. The story broke in the weekly *San Francisco Progress* in a front-page story, "Sex Deviates Make SF Headquarters." Thus DOB might dissolve out of fear. The meeting was heavily attended, and the sentiment was overwhelming to stand our ground and to get a special edition of The Ladder out and onto the newsstands (for the first time). The mailing and membership lists were removed from the office and placed under a blanket in the back of our station wagon for the duration of the crisis.

The daily papers mentioned the story, noted Mattachine's slander suit, ran a few letters, and then dropped it completely. In the meantime, a four-page pamphlet was distributed door-to-door to remind parents of daughters of the existence of the Daughters of Bilitis. Christopher, who was no favorite of lesbians and gays, was re-elected. However, some 9,000 people who went to the polls did not vote for anyone for mayor. What we learned was that it was helpful to have a liaison with the gay male organizations so as to be aware of what they were up to. We also learned—and it has proven to be so in later years— that in times of crisis we all pull together and more of us come out.

By 1960, DOB had chapters in Los Angeles, Chicago, and New York. It had established a book and record service. The L.A. chapter produced a 45-rpm record under the DOB label featuring Lisa Ben singing parodies of "Cruising Down the Boulevard" and "Frankie and Johnnie." DOB also carried "3 Oboli to Aphrodite," the Songs of Bilitis dramatized by "Cherise," a pseudonym for a very well-known stage, radio, and screen actress.

The first national conference of the Daughters of Bilitis was held in San Francisco in 1960 in the penthouse of the Whitcomb Hotel on Market Street. Although the Mattachine Society was an avowed part of the homophile movement, it had always been billed as an organization "interested in the problems of homosexuality." But DOB's publicity release advertised "the nation's first Lesbian Convention." Hal Call, Mattachine's president, wrote that under those circumstances, he felt most Mattachine members—99 percent male—might hesitate to attend. Jaye Bell, president of the San Francisco host chapter of DOB, replied: "If the members of Mattachine were to dress properly and act with decorum no one would take them for Lesbians."

Noting that a few clergymen had attended Mattachine and ONE conferences as individuals but not as representatives of a church, DOB sent a letter to the Northern California Council of Churches asking for an official speaker so as to develop a dialog with the church itself. Some weeks later, a reply came from the executive director apologizing for the delay: "We never had a request of this nature before, and quite frankly, we didn't know how to deal with it." The Reverend Fordyce Eastburn, representing the California Episcopal Diocese, was DOB's luncheon speaker. He said that homosexuals would be accepted in the church, but since homosexuality is a sin, we would be expected to change—either that or embrace celibacy. That was an opening. In 1967 the report of the Joint Committee on Homosexuality, appointed by Episcopal Bishop James A. Pike and on which Don Lucas of Mattachine and Del of DOB had served, was approved by the Diocesan Council. The Committee's recommendations included: endorsement of homosexual law reform, denunciation of entrapment of homosexuals by police and Alcoholic Beverage Control detectives, and the need for a broad sex education program for clergy and laity alike.

The DOB biennial conventions proved to be excellent vehicles for publicity focused on lesbians. The first convention in San Francisco received good press notices. It drew a visit from the Homosexual Detail of the San Francisco Police Department. The two men were primarily interested in finding out if the organization advocated dressing in clothing of the opposite sex. This being our first public appearance, the women were all wearing skirts.

During the second convention, in L.A. in 1962, Terry, president of the host chapter and self-employed, gained nationwide coverage when she was interviewed on television by Paul Coates. By the third, in New York City in 1964, *The New York Times* had relented on its taboo on the subject and sent a reporter. At the fourth, back in San Francisco, the 1966 convention opened the "Ten Days in August," a concentrated series of meetings including the second meeting of the North American Conference of Homophile Organizations (NACHO). Phyllis, as publicity director, pulled out all the stops. *The San Francisco Chronicle* ran a four-column article headlined "S.F. Greets Daughters." The Convention and Visitors Bureau provided help with registration to atone for leaving DOB out of the listing of upcoming conventions. On-the-hour spot announcements were made on two radio stations. Metromedia News taped some of the highlights of the program, and by afternoon Judge Joseph G. Kennedy's luncheon speech was on the air. Television stations did taped interviews and newspapers covered the event, which featured speakers from all branches of San Francisco's city government (including an official representing Mayor John Shelley, albeit the public health director).

Gay male organizations in the 50's and 60's dealt mostly with criminal law and the excesses of law enforcement: gay bar raids; sex in public toilets and parks; entrapment by undercover officers; and police brutality. DOB shared their advocacy of the American Law Institute's Model Penal Code, which would make sexual activity between consenting adults in private no longer a concern of the law. But the Daughters, the only national lesbian organization at the time, concentrated more on civil law and family issues.

In January 1957, DOB announced the formation of a group to discuss the problems of "raising children in a deviant relationship." Suffragist Rhoda Kellogg, director of Golden Gate Nursery School, Eleanor van Leeuwen, specialist in parent education for the San Francisco Unified School District, and Faith Rossiter, psychotherapist, participated as discussion moderators, lending assistance on the basis of their knowledge and experience. In her report of the first meeting, Jean Peterson, writing in *The Ladder*, pointed out that "anything which strays from the sincere feeling or true values can be said to be deviant, and there can definitely be deviant heterosexuals as well as deviant homophiles. The emotional stability of parents will determine the background of the child. Love and security overshadow all other factors. If a child knows love, gives love and receives love, and knows he is wanted, chances are he will be normal and well-adjusted."

The last national conference of the DOB was held in New York City in 1970. Since Rita LaPorte, then national president of DOB, feared she would not be re-elected, and Gene Damon (Barbara Grier) feared she would not be re-appointed by the new board of directors, they stole the mailing list and, in effect, *The Ladder*. Without a magazine to publish, the convention decided to dissolve the national structure. Chapters would be autonomous, could publish their own magazine, and hopefully would still come together biennially. *The Ladder*, without an organization behind it, went out of business in 1972.

Lawrence v. Texas Brings It All Back Home

JOHN RECHY

IN STRIKING DOWN the Texas law that made consensual sex in private between members of the same sex a criminal act, Justice Anthony M. Kennedy, speaking for the majority of the Supreme Court, wrote that the Texas law "demeans the lives of homosexual persons ... entitled to respect for their private lives." By emphasizing the word "respect," Justice Kennedy was not only upholding the right of privacy, he was asserting human dignity. For many, it is difficult to feel grateful. That the matter came up at all is disgraceful to every concept of human decency. For veterans of not-so-long-ago battles for equal rights, the decision will stir memories of outrages survived.

In the late 1950's, the McCarthy hearings aimed at identifying Communist sympathizers had spread their poison to ferreting out homosexuals in the government. That created an exodus to California, a state always known for its liberal attitudes. Perhaps it was that new wave of homosexuals into the state that intensified entrenched prejudices—and what occurred in California was reflected in varying degrees throughout the country.

A series of sweeps on Hollywood Boulevard by police netted hundreds of homosexuals, who were stopped, harassed, even taken into police stations for further interrogation. A scurrilous Hollywood newspaper trumpeted the news: "100's of Deviants Detained, Warned." The arrests were for "loitering." Any two men sitting in a parked car on streets near the Boulevard risked being ordered out by the police, separated, and grilled with questions about each other. Such questioning was meant to determine whether or not they had just picked each other up, a signal of lewd intent. That tactic was so widespread that gay men together, on sensing the presence of the police, whether in bars or on the street, would hurriedly exchange names and brief backgrounds to suggest a friendship, as opposed to a quick connection.

Throughout the 50's and 60's, and even into the 70's, being in a gay bar was dangerous. At any moment a bar could be flooded with light from a squad car. A bullhorn ordered all "queers" to march out in a single line, ostensibly to be checked for ID. Gay men would be insulted, mauled, and in some instances beaten. As many men as could be fitted into a squad car or wagon were taken to headquarters for questioning. Anyone who protested would be threatened with being held on "open suspicion" for 48 hours, released, rearrested, and held again.

Since it was illegal for members of the same sex to dance together (heterosexual women were exempted), a "private" club in Topanga Canyon adopted a system of lights to signal a hostile presence. Bulbs would blink and partners would shift, with gay men dancing with lesbians. The illegality of gay men touching each other even while dancing produced the Madison, a dance during which lines of gay men faced each other, not touching, just going through the motions of a dance.

In 1968, the murder of silent film star Ramon Novarro by two young drifters resulted in the trial not only of the killers but of the star's life. Newspapers all over the country routinely quoted the defense lawyers' reference to the silent-film star as "an old queer." The fact that his murder was brought to trial and the killers convicted was exceptional, occurring mainly because of Novarro's one-time fame. Other incidents of violence against gay people, even murder, were left uninvestigated, even unreported, since it was known that in courtrooms, if the perpetrator of violence against a gay man claimed he had responded in anger at having been the object of a homosexual pass, he would be assured a not guilty verdict.

Plainclothes cops would sit in cars outside gay gathering places in order to trail men leaving together. Without warrants, they pushed their way into private homes, just as, years later, the Texas police would invade a private home and arrest two men in the Lawrence case. Men caught in such situations often went to prison; a sentence of up to five years was not rare.

Entrapment was rampant. Vice cops dressed in the tight white pants popular at one time might, while hanging out in a gay bar or on the street, court or accept an invitation for sex at someone's home, and then arrest the gay man for solicitation. In 1965, a man attempting his first gay encounter was arrested in Twentynine Palms, California, after a plainclothes cop struck up a conversation that led to a mutual agreement to go to a motel. The gay man was sentenced to six months in jail, where he remained incommunicado, the judge claiming he was "insane" and needed to be "scrutinized." After he managed to get out, he became a recluse, petrified for life by the incident.

Countless lives were destroyed by such arrests: men lost their jobs, were ostracized by their families, were threatened with electric shock treatment, ordered to stay away from any place catering to "perverts"—in effect sentenced to a life of loneliness, away from their own kind. All men convicted of a gay sex offense had to register for life as "sex offenders." As such, they were frequently summoned out of their homes at night to participate in lineups for unrelated offenses, heterosexual rape, or child molestation.

Fledgling political groups, such as the Mattachine Society, met in secret, their blinds drawn. Their newsletters—mimeographed sheets—were confiscated by the Post Office even though they had no erotic content. Such a fate awaited the first gay activist magazine, *One,* which was entirely non-erotic.

In 1973, hundreds of gay men in Griffith Park were rounded up, not on hidden trails where sexual encounters occurred, but simply as they walked along on open roads or gathered publicly around their cars, a traditional gay practice on a warm Sunday afternoon. Suddenly a helicopter, a fleet of squad cars, and more than a dozen police on horses launched an invasion, proceeding to herd dozens of gay men into a wired compound at the foot of the roads. The routed men were kept in the compound for several hours, names and addresses were checked out, and 39 were taken to police headquarters for booking. Those who were released from the compound had to trudge up the miles of road to their cars. Those taken to the station had to abandon their cars along the darkening roads. *The Advocate* (at that time a small newspaper) described the maneuver as "a full scale military operation, with command post, detention buses, jeeps, a helicopter, marked and unmarked cops, uniformed and vice police ... and a contingent of mounted cops," concluding that it was "a new harassment strategy." The Los Angeles Times reported only that "39 men ... were cited ... for possible prosecution under city ordinances, prohibiting sections designated as hazardous. ... They could face penalties of up to one year in jail and a $500 fine."

On an early evening in 1977—four years after the repeal of California's anti-sodomy laws—while driving home from UCLA, I saw muggers fleeing from a man they had assaulted on the street as he walked home with his groceries along a non-gay area. I stopped to be sure that the man was okay: he was bruised and shaken. With him in my car, I attempted to flag down a squad car in the area. Hands readied on their revolvers, the cops got out. The muggers would still be in the area, I told them. Glancing at the wounded man, who was clearly gay, they drove off. I took the bruised man to the police station to report the crime. The desk sergeant studied him knowingly. "What did you try to do with those guys?" he asked.

After I wrote an account of that night for *The L.A. Times*, and an investigation was ordered because the matter was now public and no gay context had been indicated, I became the object of retaliation, culminating in an attack by baton-swinging cops in Barnsdall Park, a cruising area I often frequented. As I got out of my car, two cops rushed at me with batons raised. I was able to get back into my car and speed toward them. As I drove past, they swung their batons in an action intended for me. I heard the sickening strikes on my car, leaving deep dents. For months afterward, I received threatening anonymous calls.

In 1983, a vice cop and his plainclothes partner, having made an entrapment arrest for lewd conduct in Griffith Park, lingered along the main road with a handcuffed gay man as a trophy until other gay men had gathered. Summoning a park ranger, the arresting cop asked loudly: "Think anyone would mind if I set fire to this part of the park to burn these faggots?" Intending to bring that statement into the court hearing as indicative of the cop's vengeful intent to entrap, the city attorney prosecuting the case said he did not believe that an officer would say that, nor would any judge or jury accept it. The statement was not introduced, and the entrapped gay man was convicted.

There was resistance throughout those years in Los Angeles,

however. As early as 1958, as the cops pursued a routine, hour-long harassing tactic of checking IDs at a crowded after-hours gathering place for gay men, Cooper's Donuts on Main Street, the men inside pushed en masse past the cops, and a violent rumble ensued. After the notorious raid on the Black Cat Bar in 1967, riotous disruptions against the police spread to L.A., where 200 gay men marched against a line of heavily armed cops. In early 1969, the nearly fatal beating of a gay man in downtown L.A. created skirmishes and demonstrations sporadically for days.

But the same prejudices that allowed myriad outrages against gay people caused these acts to be ignored by the mainstream press. Unacknowledged, their insurrectionary power was curbed.

Although the history of gay oppression is long, its recorded history is brief. For many gay men, history begins with the moment of their last sexual conquest. Many younger homosexuals have no knowledge about what occurred not so long ago—and still occurs away from relatively safe havens, those deceptive gay ghettos. It could all have returned ferociously as long as repressive laws like the one in Texas existed.

On the memorable day of June 25, 2003, in decent, moving words, Justice Kennedy and the four justices who joined him in effect denounced those past horrors as inconsistent with the respect and dignity owed to all human beings. Without in any way belittling the decency of those justices in their opinion—and the courage and commitment of those who fought to bring it about, especially the Lambda Legal Defense Fund and its attorneys—many gay people might view the decision as a vastly imperfect apology for the lives devastated by cruel laws that made possible the myriad humiliations of gay people, the verbal and physical assaults, the screams of "faggot!"—the muggings, the suicides, the murders, trumped-up arrests, incarceration—still occurring even during this time of victory.

The flagrant dissent by Justice Scalia and two of his colleagues—in an effort to uphold the Texas law—will help to keep fertile the atmosphere of hatred that recently allowed three men to mangle Trevor Broudy in West Hollywood and two others to butcher Matthew Shepard in Wyoming. A great battle was won on June 25, but the war continues.

Unearthing the 'Knights of the Clock'

MARTHA E. STONE

IN his letter to the editor in the January-February 2010 issue of this magazine, Richard Lottridge asked if anything had been written about the role of Merton L. Bird in the founding of the mid-century gay Los Angeles group known as Knights of the Clock. My interest was piqued, and what follows is a brief overview in which I've tried to assemble some (often contradictory) fragments of history.

Enigmatic might be the best word to describe this organization, which was variously called the Knights of the Clock or Clocks. Gay and lesbian historians differ in their reporting of who founded the group, when it was founded, and what its exact name was. The ONE Gay and Lesbian Archives in L.A. maintains that Merton L. Bird, an African-American accountant about whom little is known, was the cofounder, and that it started up around June 1951. The other co-founder was W. Dorr Legg, who used about a dozen pseudonyms throughout his life, and whose name appears in virtually every anthology of gay history. He earned a master's degree in landscape architecture with a specialty in urban planning, taught at Oregon State University, lived in New York and Florida, and came home to Ann Arbor, Michigan, to care for his elderly parents. Most of Legg's lovers were African-American, and he experienced racial discrimination firsthand (though not, according to John D'Emilio in 1983's *Sexual Politics, Sexual Communities*, in Detroit's black community). Some historians hold that Bird and Legg met in Michigan, drove around looking for a comfortable place for interracial gay couples, and landed in L.A. in the late 1940s. Lillian Faderman and Stuart Timmons hold in *Gay L.A.* (2006) that Marvin Edwards, not Bird, went to L.A. with Legg. Timmons interviewed Edwards for the book, which includes a very youthful candid photo. Edwards was forced to leave L.A. after a year or so, when his landlady discovered he was gay.

Legg has been variously described as charismatic, charming, poised, witty, intelligent, controlling, inflexible, and opinionated. A Republican in politics, he chose to live off the earnings of younger men (according to an interview in Joseph Hansen's 1998 biography of Don Slater). In Legg's 1994 book, *Homophile Studies in Theory and Practice*, he described Bird as brilliant and gives all credit for the Knights' founding to Bird. "Hostility and harassment were the daily lot of interracial same-sex couples in 1950. ... [Bird's] idea was that by coming together to form a mutual aid society, the group could at the very least offer each other encouragement. The decision was to form a California nonprofit corporation and call it the Knights of the Clocks, a deliberately ambiguous title." Many historians have quoted from Legg's book, *Homosexuals Today; A Handbook of Organizations & Publications* (1956), which he wrote under the name of Marvin Cutler, stating that the aim of the Knights was to "promote fellowship and understanding between homosexuals themselves, specifically between other races and the Negro, as well as to offer its members aid in securing employment and suitable housing. Special attention was given to the housing problems of interracial couples of which there were several in the group."

Although most sources give June 1951 as the Knights' founding date, others range from the late 1940s to the early '50s. Perhaps the L.A. group known as the Cloistered Loyal Order of the Conclaved Knights of Sophisticracy (or, sometimes, Sophistocracy, and known as the C.L.O.C.K.S.) inspired the name of Bird and Legg's organization. It may or may not have been formally incorporated. In *Gay American History* (1976), Jonathan Ned Katz was unable to turn up the legal papers when he searched back in the 1970s, but Edward Sagarin (the pseudonym of Donald Webster Cory) states in what was originally his NYU thesis, later published as *Structure and Ideology in an Association of Deviants* (1966), that the Knights incorporated in 1950. Three undated typescripts in the ONE Archives' file on the Knights contain some information about the C.L.O.C.K.S. Their oath of office, following a Masonic-type ritual, was to "practice the arts of sophisticracy diligently, honestly, courteously, amicably, faithfully, and with all of my ability." At the end of the installation, the installing officer and "honor guard" intoned: "By the authority vested in me by the State of California, and as a duly elected officer of this corporation, I hereby declare you [name of office]. Honi soit qui mal y pense." This, the motto of the Order of the Garter, founded in mid-14th-century England, can be roughly translated as "shamed be he who thinks evil of it." Instead of the usual titles (president, VP, etc.), the C.L.O.C.K.S. used medieval ones: Exalted Knight, Senior Knight, Bursar, and Scribe (who kept a Tablet instead of minutes).

In the ONE archive, a few handwritten entries beginning on May 24, 1951, were recorded in an unused 1944 calendar from what appears to be an insurance company. On that date, "application forms were passed out," "minutes were approved as read," and the "Vice President spoke of aims of Club." Gone is the mystique of the Cloistered Loyal Order. One of the Knights' events was planned to take place in June at the Wilfandel Club. According to the still-active club's website, wilfandelclub.com, it was established on November 21, 1945, by two black women to provide "people of all races with a public meeting place in Los Angeles during the 1950s." Another meeting note, dated July 1st, listed members who would sing, play an instrument, dance, and make speeches at an upcoming party. (Bird was listed as one of the speech-makers.) On that same date, there was an entry for a rough draft of letterhead, "The C.L.O.C.K.S. / Incorporated / Los Angeles / Calif." The name "Josephine Baker" appears fleetingly in a meeting note, leaving one to imagine all kinds of possibilities.

Yet another event, dated August 4th, was to be a "midsummer frolic" beginning at 9 p.m., with draft beer and spaghetti. The last social event mentioned was a Valentine's meeting with a "social program" planned for Saturday, February 16th, 1952. Events seemed to be admission-by-card only. Other cryptic entries mentioned the Loan Fund, Housing & Employment Committee, the Membership Committee, the Entertainment Committee, and the Legal Aid Committee, of which Bird was chair. "NAACP" is noted without any further comment. Interestingly, Bird's name is consistently spelled "Byrd," and C. Todd White's 2009 book *Pre-Gay L.A.* lists "M. Byrd" as Merton Bird's pseudonym. Some members' names and addresses are written throughout the entries, and there's an intriguing mention of a seal and articles of incorporation. Sagarin remarked that meetings were originally held monthly, then semi-monthly. Meetings, he said, usually drew about 35 attendees, with a larger group attending the socials.

Reproduced in Legg's 1994 book and credited to "ONE's Baker Memorial Library and Archives" is a 1951 invitation, engraved in Gothic script, to a Knights social event: the fourth anniversary party of "Gene and Edward" on May 12, 1951, from 9 p.m. to 3 a.m. Legg stated that guests at that event were "a comfortable mix of races and assorted personal relationships including both men's Beverly Hills employers and their families." ONE Archives' handwritten meeting notes do include some female first names.

When did the end come? ONE Archives' file contains no information about the group beyond a handwritten list, dated February 15, 1952, of fourteen members (including Bird and Legg) who owed dues. On that date, the group had $14.15 in the bank. In 1952, Legg and Bird numbered among the founders of *ONE*, Inc., a group within the Mattachine Society that published *One* magazine. White mentions that Bird appeared to have offered the Knights' charter as a model, or offered to merge with the Knights, neither of which was accepted. Sagarin noted that "for all practical purposes it had disappeared from the scene" by 1953, though an occasional meeting was held after that date.

A 1966 article in *Tangents* magazine by Richard Conger implied that the Knights, "formerly of Los Angeles," were represented at the ONE Institute Midwinter Session, an educational program for gay men and lesbians held on an almost yearly basis in various cities and considered a precursor to today's academic programs. The Institute was the brainchild of Legg. Sidney Rothman reported of the Knights (in *One* magazine, 1965): "Its originality lay in its avowed intention to enroll men and women alike and their parents and other relatives on an interracial basis. Its meetings and large social gatherings appear not to have been matched in attendance until this present year (1965) by a few social events staged in San Francisco as the joint effort of several homophile organizations in that city. The Knights continued for three or four years but eventually found themselves overshadowed by another Los Angeles development ... the Mattachine." (Conger and Rothman were, according to Vern Bullough in 2002's *Before Stonewall*, two of Legg's pseudonyms.)

When Legg died in 1994 at the age of 89, he was survived by

his partner of over thirty years, John (Johnny) Nojima, who died a few years ago. Very little is known at this time about Merton L. Bird. ONE's file contains the names and addresses of some of the earliest Knights. Can any of them be traced? Are any of their addresses close to those noted on the map of "significant locations" in Todd White's book? What might the archives of other California institutions contain? Did any of the Knights' files migrate to other gay organizations following a very celebrated "heist" of papers in 1965 by another ONE, Inc. founder, Don Slater, due to personal and professional disputes with Legg? Does the NAACP's L.A. chapter keep records back to the 1950s? What about the archives of the Wilfandel Club? More research is waiting to be done on this fascinating and pioneering organization.

Hitchcock's cameo comes early in The Birds.

From: March–April 2001

The Birds as a Pre-Stonewall Parable

BOB SMITH

IN one of the coming attraction trailers for Alfred Hitchcock's film, *The Birds*, Tippi Hedren screams, "They're coming! They're coming!" She's warning that a bird attack is imminent, but after seeing the film again recently—an interim of twenty years—I began to wonder if she was actually predicting the Stonewall riots and the approach of Gay Pride marchers. I first saw *The Birds* as a boy in Buffalo, but after seeing the film as an adult, it struck me that *The Birds* could be a parody of homophobia, for there are entire sections of dialogue in the film where the phrase "The Birds" could easily be replaced by "The Gays."

The Birds opens in San Francisco, where we glimpse Alfred Hitchcock making his traditional cameo appearance, this time as a big queen walking two prissy little dogs [photo at left]. He passes by Tippi Hedren's character, Melanie Daniels, as she enters a pet store, where she meets Mitch Brenner, played by Rod Taylor. Mitch wants to buy a pair of lovebirds for his sister's birthday, but after meeting, flirting, and arguing with Melanie, he departs the store without his gift. Smitten by the hunky Mitch, the infatuated Melanie impulsively decides to order a pair of lovebirds and deliver them to him the following day. Using her father's connections as the publisher of one of San Francisco's newspapers, she tracks down Mitch's address and is about to leave the cage and a letter outside his apartment door, when she learns from the queen who lives across the hall (played by a gay man, the famous character actor Richard Deacon) that Mitch has already gone to Bodega Bay to visit his mother for the weekend.

If we sex-change Melanie Daniels into Daniel Melanie, we have a story about a blond boy toy chasing a ruggedly handsome young daddy. Driving up to Bodega Bay in her snazzy silver convertible to deliver the lovebirds, Melanie ends up staying the weekend with Annie, the town's school teacher. Since this film was made in an era when seemingly no gay man was complete without his gal-pal (who had a hopeless crush), Annie turns out to be a boozy, chain-smoking "fag-hag" played by Suzanne Pleshette, her husky voice beginning its descent to the register in which it sounds as if her larynx is a piece of smoked and pickled salmon. Puffing away on a cigarette, Annie admits to Melanie that she moved to Bodega Bay just to be near Mitch, and goes on to question his heterosexuality by suggesting, "Maybe there's never been anything between Mitch and any girl." Reflecting upon her remark, Annie says, "I think I'll have some of that," and reaches to help herself to a glass of brandy; and the viewer can almost imagine the heartsick school teacher embarking upon a lifetime of solitary drinking. It's a sad and pathetic confession, and since the audience grows to like the sympathetic Annie, it's almost a relief when, later in the film, she gets bumped off by a flock of crows instead of spending the rest of her life pining for a guy that she'll never have.

Mitch is still a "bachelor." And since the film was made in 1963, it comes as no surprise that he has a domineering mother, played superbly by Jessica Tandy. Mitch's mom is a controlling sort who disapproves of everyone he brings home and openly worries that he might leave her. Twisted mother-son relationships were a subject that obviously fascinated Hitchcock, and I like to think that if the Bates Motel had been located in Bodega Bay, Mitch and Norman might have met and become boyfriends.

It has always been clear that *The Birds* is about "the birds and the bees." The arrival of Melanie, a bad girl who reportedly jumped naked into a fountain in Rome, coincides with the attacks by the birds. In the restaurant scene where the birds attack a gas station attendant, and a dropped match in the flowing gasoline causes a conflagration, a mother attacks Melanie in terms that could easily be used by homophobic nutjobs. "They said when you got here the whole thing started. Who are you? What are you? Where did you come from? I think you're the cause of all this. I think you're evil. Evil!"

In response, Melanie slaps the hysterical woman, an action

that most homophobes deserve but few ever receive. The woman's question, "Where are you from?", is significant because, throughout the film, San Francisco is presented as a locus of evil. Whenever one of Bodega Bay's citizens mentions San Francisco, you can almost hear the disapproval in their voice. Of course, San Francisco has always had a raffish reputation, but since World War II the city has been regarded by some as a Sodom and Gomorrah where odd birds of a certain feather go to flock together.

The first major attack by the birds is at Mitch's younger sister's birthday party. The girl is played by the young Veronica Cartwright, who in *The Birds* discovered what would become her specialty as an actor, the portrayal of hysterical women. (Tears and panic have become the bread and butter of Miss Cartwright's career. Since her appearance in *The Birds*, she's screamed in Philip Kaufman's wonderful 1977 remake of *Invasion of the Body Snatchers*, shrieked in *Alien*, and, in surely her most memorable performance, projectile cherry-vomited in *The Witches of Eastwick*.) In the movie, the birds are consistently portrayed as predators on children, a libel that has also been employed against The Gays. Hitchcock even goes so far as to suggest that the birds are lurking pedophiles stalking schoolchildren in the playground. In fact, the birds in the film seem to be truly evil queens, since the two people killed by the birds, Annie and a chicken farmer, are shown to have had their eyes scratched out.

Once the attacks begin, the residents of Bodega Bay have a difficult time accepting the idea that birds could ever become violent. After the attack at the birthday party, the sheriff dismisses the evidence that birds attacked people, and in the restaurant Mrs. Bundy—an ornithologist who, to all outward appearances, is the epitome of a butch lesbian—says: "Birds are not aggressive creatures. They bring beauty into the world." Mrs. Bundy goes on to suggest that if birds started flocking together, "We wouldn't have a chance. How could we hope to fight them?" It's probable that Mrs. Bundy and the sheriff would have voiced the same incredulity if someone had suggested that in a few years drag queens would fight back against the New York City police or that, a decade later, the nearby town of Guerneville on the Russian River would be a gay resort.

It's a shame that Hitchcock didn't stick with his original ending for the film. The last scene of *The Birds* shows Mitch, Melanie, his mother, and his sister driving off into the distance, but Hitchcock had planned another ending that would have been more memorable while continuing the homophobic subtext. Hitchcock was going to show their car arriving at the Golden Gate Bridge, which, to their horror, would be covered with perching birds. It would have made explicit what people have been saying for years about San Francisco: "They've taken over the city!"

Frank Kameny leads march at Independence Hall, Philadelphia, July 4, 1966

Frank Kameny Takes It Public

JOHN D'EMILIO

FRANK Kameny's death last fall has pushed me to think about historical reputation. How do we evaluate the lives of those in the broad GLBT community who have assumed public roles, particularly in the world of political activism? Who gets memorialized? Who gets remembered as a hero? What achievements bring recognition on the historical record card?

Mainstream history books offer little guidance, as they still largely ignore queer topics. While our movement certainly exists in popular consciousness, it seems leaderless and in that sense different from other movements for social justice. For instance, in the long history of the black freedom struggle, at least a few individuals have won a secure place in the historical ledger as larger-than-life figures. Names like Frederick Douglass, Sojourner Truth, W.E.B. Du Bois, Martin Luther King, Jr., and Malcolm X have wide recognition. Mention "suffrage" and "feminism" and, at the very least, women such as Elizabeth Cady Stanton, Susan B. Anthony, and Betty Friedan pop to mind.

But turn to our movement for sexual and gender justice, and the cupboard seems bare. I've heard claims made for Harvey Milk as the most important person in our movement's history. But, I think, really? He was a local elected official for eleven months before being assassinated. Then there was Harry Hay, the founder of the Mattachine Society. Sure, he got something started, quit after two years when the going got tough, and then occasionally showed up later at Radical Faerie gatherings. Or Christine Jorgensen, who had very high visibility in the popular culture of her time, to be sure; but the coverage of her almost always took on the tone of freak-show reportage.

In the days after Frank Kameny's death, there was lots of discussion on the web and on various e-mail lists about his place in history. The range of views was extraordinary. Some described him in dismissive tones as just one among many, while others christened him the greatest GLBT hero of all time, bar none. As activists go, Kameny has at least fared well in the published histories of the movement. Oral history narratives like those of Eric Marcus and Paul Cain include a chapter on him. My own overview of pre-Stonewall activism paints him as one of two or three key figures pressing the movement in more militant, assertive directions in the 1960s. In *The Lavender Scare,* a study of the Cold War persecutions in Washington, David Johnson makes him a central agent of change. Kameny figures in Clendenin and Nagourney's journalistic survey of the gay and lesbian movement, 2013's *Out for Good,* and in Ronald Bayer's account of how the American Psychiatric Association came to eliminate homosexuality from its list of mental illnesses (*Homosexuality and American Psychiatry,* 1981).

In an effort to think through the question of reputation, and of Kameny's in particular, I went back to the research I did in the 1970s, a time so close to the events most associated with his public career that it could barely be considered history. I pulled out the text of speeches he gave and letters he wrote, documents that in the 1970s were still housed in his and other activists' filing cabinets. I also found the notes I took during an interview with him that I did in 1978.

Born in 1925 in New York City, Franklin Kameny was a Harvard-educated astronomer working for the federal government in 1957. He had every reason to believe, at the dawn of the space age, that not even the sky was a limit to his career possibilities. But the Feds found evidence of his homosexuality and, at a time when "sex perversion" made someone unemployable by both the government and any of its contractors, Kameny was fired and had no prospects of ever finding work in his field again. He appealed the decision, all the way to the Supreme Court, losing at every stage.

When these avenues of redress failed, he decided to fight in a different way. With some friends he founded the Mattachine Society of Washington (MSW). Over the next fifteen years, he fought tirelessly to change federal policy. He organized the first homosexual rights demonstrations in Washington. He got the ACLU to take on gay rights issues. He challenged the ban on federal employment in every way feasible. He took on the medical establishment's claim that homosexuality was an illness, and coined the slogan "gay is good." In 1971, he ran as an openly gay candidate to be the District of Columbia's non-voting representative in Congress. He helped found and served on the board of the National Gay Task Force, an early, and successful, effort to create a national activist organization. By the mid-1970s, Kameny had the satisfaction of seeing two of his core goals achieved when the American Psychiatric Association voted to declassify homosexuality as a disease and the Civil Service Commission dropped its blanket ban on the employment of gays, lesbians, and bisexuals.

It would be hard to claim that Kameny continued to be a key mover and shaker after the mid-70s. However, he never ceased being an activist, and he always did much behind the scenes that was unheralded. He freely made himself available to individuals who experienced police harassment, lost their jobs, or faced blackmail because of their homosexuality. Later in life, other activists used Kameny's career, with his permission, as a way of winning additional recognition from the federal government. His house is a D.C. historic landmark. The Library of Congress has acquired his papers. The Smithsonian Museum has displayed some of his activist memorabilia. The federal government has formally issued an apology for firing him.

On what grounds can Kameny's activism be seen as singularly significant? For starters, through MSW he charted a whole new direction for homophile organizations. Evaluating where this small movement was in the early 1960s, he astutely characterized its work as either "social service" or "information and education." In his view, neither promised much in the way of permanent change. Instead, drawing explicitly on the civil rights movement and the huge changes its public activism was achieving, he proposed an emphasis on what he called "civil liberties and social action." Forget helping those individuals in need. Forget soothing efforts at educating and persuading the oppressor. Having tried unsuccessfully to win back his job with reasoned argument, Kameny now saw the opposition as "a ruthless, unscrupulous foe" with a "prejudiced mind ... not penetrated by information." To an audience of Mattachine members and sympathizers in New York, he urged "bold, strong, uncompromising initiative."

In practice, this translated into a series of actions that moved beyond what homophile organizations customarily did. He pushed back against a right-wing member of Congress who targeted MSW. He sent a steady stream of letters to government officials demanding meetings. Most of all, he and those who shared this more assertive outlook took to the sidewalks of the nation's capital. With large picket signs that boldly identified their issue as equal rights for homosexuals, they marched in front of the White House and other government buildings. Kameny eagerly talked to the journalists who flocked to the startling scene of homosexuals unapologetically proclaiming their cause.

Besides the federal government, Kameny aggressively took on the psychiatrists and their disease classification of homosexuality. In the past, Mattachine and the Daughters of Bilitis had reached out to medical and mental health professionals, but the approach was to win them over as allies and then support their efforts at new scientific research to challenge the sickness model. At its best, this approach led to the kind of work that Dr. Evelyn Hooker, a social psychologist, began producing in the late 1950s. Kameny was having none of this. He was not relying on experts. "I take the position unequivocally," he declared, that homosexuality "is neither a sickness, a defect, a disturbance, a neurosis, a psychosis, nor a malfunction of any sort." He went further. Taking on religion as well as science and law, he staked out new ground: "We cannot ask for our rights from a position of inferiority, or from a position, shall I say, as less than whole human beings." To Kameny this meant that homosexual acts between consenting adults had to be defended as "moral, in a positive and real sense" and as "right, good and desirable, both for the individual participants and for the society in which they live."

MILITANCY and pride—stances that seem so obvious today. They are the foundation upon which the gains of the post-Stonewall decades stand. But when Kameny first articulated these principles, they represented the frontiers of GLBT political thought. What allowed him to stake out that ground so fearlessly? Was it an intellectual confidence gained from having a doctorate from Harvard? Was it the happenstance of personality? Kameny was notoriously brash, sharp-edged, and prickly. He didn't care if his words offended someone. He could come across as tough as nails, unsparing in his assessment of others, and unburdened by self-doubt. He seems to have escaped the internalized sense of inferiority that oppression often breeds.

One of my favorite statements of Kameny comes from a letter he wrote to a New York activist in 1965, the year in which he launched the Washington demonstrations: "I have always said that the world will take me on MY own terms, or it won't get me, and the world's loss will be greater than will mine; that when the world and I differ, I am right and the world is wrong and that if one of us or the other MUST change, it will be the world, because I won't." Can one imagine a stance better suited to a society in which all things queer were reviled, marginalized, or punished?

Kameny was not, of course, alone in his work. The positions that he espoused were enthusiastically embraced by a core of other activists, and the actions that he proposed came to fruition because others took them up, side by side with him. People like Jack Nichols, Barbara Gittings, Craig Rodwell, Randy Wicker, and Lilli Vincenz were among his partners in crime in the 1960s. But there's no doubt that Kameny was staking out the ground and that he had the will—the bull-headedness, perhaps—to keep pressing forward and to succeed in bringing others along. The launching of campaigns against the federal government and the psychiatric establishment brought the movement's biggest victories in the mid-1970s.

So maybe he is the greatest gay hero, deserving a position at the front of the pantheon. But listen to what Kameny himself had to say in an interview in 1978. Stonewall, he asserted, was "a turning point," accomplishing "what we had been trying to do for years and years and years and had never been able to do, and what we had anguished over endlessly: that the gay movement had never been a grassroots movement; it had never fired up the general gay community. Stonewall made the movement a grassroots movement."

And Stonewall itself, he believed, came not from homophile activism but from a larger impulse sweeping the country. "What happened at Stonewall was very much in keeping with the spirit of the times," he told me. "It was an era of tremendous ferment, of activism and militancy that hadn't occurred in recent historical memory. ... Riots were becoming commonplace in every part of the country. ... And then you had the whole, very active and pervasive radical community and radical philosophy, which was setting a tone for everything that went on. Stonewall happened at the right moment, and it happened because it was the right moment."

Kameny, never known for his self-effacing modesty, is telling us something important about movements, social change, and individuals. Can one imagine the doctors disavowing generations of theorizing about homosexuality without the militant disruptions of their staid conferences undertaken by this radical grassroots movement? Can one imagine the federal government retreating from their employment ban without all those disruptions of business-as-usual that the mass movements of the '60s and '70s regularly brought to Washington?

Kameny could see that the changes he espoused and the goals he pursued were not about to be achieved until something else of consequence was added to the stew of social change: the energy and strength of mobilized communities, of populations in open revolt. A leader without many followers is not the recipe for permanent change. Kameny never could figure out how to create those armies of lovers clamoring for justice.

Kameny deserves a place in the historical record. He did make a difference in important ways. He is neither just one among the many, nor is he the one without whom the changes that we take for granted today would not have occurred. Kameny himself, I suspect, would be quite happy with such a spare and respectful assessment of his contribution. As he told Eric Marcus just over twenty years ago: "my life has been more exciting and stimulating and interesting and satisfying and rewarding and fulfilling than I ever could possibly have dreamed it would be." He knew he had done right by himself and the world.

The Black Cat Riot in L.A.

EVE GOLDBERG

IT'S the final hour of the year 1966. In Hollywood, a radio deejay sets down the needle on the number eight song of the year. "I love the colorful clothes she wears/ And the way the sunlight plays upon her hair." A few miles away, in Silverlake, things are hopping at the Black Cat. Colored balloons cover the ceiling. Boys dance with boys, the jukebox wails, and a couple of undercover cops play pool over in the corner. Six or seven additional plain-clothes officers mill around in the crowd. At 11:30, a gaggle of glittering drag queens arrives in full-blown bouffants, sequins, and wobbly spiked heels. The bartender cranks up the Supremes' "You Can't Hurry Love."

The Black Cat is one of about a dozen gay bars lining Sunset Boulevard in Silverlake, the heart of L.A.'s gay community in the 1960s. Many are beer bars with jukeboxes, pool tables, and pinball machines, inhabiting rundown buildings where the rents were cheap.

It's just a few minutes before midnight on New Year's Eve at the Black Cat, and the Rhythm Queens, a trio of black women singers hired for the night, are getting ready for their big number. Suddenly, the jukebox cuts off, and for a brief moment all that can be heard is the tinkle of champagne glasses. All eyes are riveted on the clock behind the bar. Then a cheer goes up. "Happy New Year!" The Rhythm Queens take their cue, belting out a jazzy "Auld Lang Syne." The bartender snips a string and the balloons cascade down onto dozens of kissing couples.

The undercover cops exchange nods. Without warning, one officer seizes a kissing customer by the shoulders. "You're under arrest!" He pushes the man to the ground. Another cop grabs the bartender. Wine glasses shatter, Christmas decorations come crashing down. Patrons scream with fear, running for the exits. One customer reaches out to open the front door. The butt-end of a pool cue cracks down on his head. Blood spurts from his ear as it splits open. Another man is flung head-first against the jukebox.

Moments later, a dozen uniformed cops from the Los Angeles Police Department charge into the bar, batons swinging. One patron is clubbed from behind, then kneed in the groin. As he falls to the floor, his bowels empty. Two panicked customers rush out the back door, seeking refuge in the New Faces bar just across the street. A couple of plain-clothes officers follow. Just inside the New Faces, the fleeing men are tackled and thrown to the ground. Shocked, the female bar owner comes forward. "Can I see some identification?" she asks the plainclothes officers. In response, one of the cops hits her, then shoves her to the floor. A cop seizes the bartender, Robert Haas, and yanks him across the bar. Haas is struck, dragged out onto the sidewalk, and beaten so severely that his spleen ruptures. He doubles over, going unconscious on the way down.

NEW Year's Day, 1967, was another sunny day in L.A. Motorized carts draped in luscious mantels of carnations, daisies, and of course roses glided up Colorado Boulevard in the Rose Parade. Millions of snow-bound Americans were glued to their TVs, watching host Pat Boone chat with *Bewitched* star Elizabeth Montgomery as the floats floated beneath a cloudless sky. Over at L.A. County General Hospital, bartender Robert Haas was in critical condition with a ruptured spleen. At LAPD's Parker Center, fourteen Black Cat customers have been booked for lewd behavior. Their crime? Kissing for more than three seconds.

Local businessman Alexei Romanoff was not happy. "I wasn't at the Black Cat that night," he later said, "but within hours I heard about the raid. I was absolutely irate. I got on the phone with friends. Everybody was angry. We talked about making a plan to express our outrage." Romanoff had once been an owner of the New Faces bar. Working as a nurse and pursuing an acting career on the side, he was also intimately involved in the gay bar scene. "In the 1950s and '60s, gay bar culture was a crucial part of our community. It was a place to meet new people, maybe even meet a partner," explained Romanoff. "Police raids at gay bars were common at that time. So were beatings and arrests. It was really scary. We were so vulnerable. Kissing was a crime; cross-dressing was a crime. If you were arrested and identified as being gay, you could lose your job, your income, your house, your family."

I met Alexei in 2010 at his beautifully renovated, mid-century ranch house high in the hills of Pasadena. Sliding glass doors at the back of the house let in abundant sunlight and a sweeping view of the Los Angeles basin. Alexei and his life partner, David Farah, greeted me. It has been 43 years since the Black Cat riot. Alexei is now 74 and retired. "I've shrunk three inches," he admits with an impish grin, but he's still energetic, outspoken, and every bit the passionate activist who played a role in the course of gay American history.

"Before the Black Cat raid, gays were usually meek and scared. If we were arrested, we'd cop to a lesser charge like disorderly conduct so we wouldn't have to register as a sex offender for the rest of our lives. We just wanted to be left alone. But that night, something changed." What changed was that gay people fought back. Two and a half years before the famous Stonewall riots in New York City, they came out of the closet and into the streets of L.A.

"Perhaps it was the reeking mass brutality of this raid that did it," wrote Jim Kepner in the February 1967 issue of *Concern*, one of the few gay periodicals in the country at the time. "Or it may have been the slow, cumulative effect of years of hard work by small, struggling organizations telling homophiles that they could fight back—and wondering all the while if anyone was listening."

"Remember," says Alexei, "it was 1967. The anti-war protests were going on. Martin Luther King and the civil rights protests were happening. I had marched for black rights, and now I'm thinking: What about us? What about our civil rights?" Indeed the idea of civil rights for gays had been slowly building within the gay community for years, and L.A. was ground zero for much of the pioneering activism that led the way. The first gay political organization in the nation, the Mattachine Society, was founded in L.A. in 1950 by the left-wing activist Harry Hay and a few of his friends. The Mattachine Society's goals were to change the public perception of gays from sexual deviants to an oppressed minority, to end anti-gay discrimination, and to raise their own personal and political awareness through consciousness-raising discussion groups. In 1954, the Mattachine's magazine *One*, which was the first gay publication in the country, fought a court battle all the way to the Supreme Court to be able to send their magazine through the mail.

In 1966, a new gay organization was formed in L.A. PRIDE (Personal Rights in Defense and Education) was more radical, militant, and youth-oriented than previous gay political groups. PRIDE's founder, Steve Ginsberg, a young landscape designer, was one of the people who organized the response to the Black Cat raid. Alexei explains how this was accomplished: "There was no Internet back then. All we had was the telephone. So I called ten people, and they called ten people. And they called ten more. We looked around for a place to meet. There was one bar owner who was brave enough to let us meet during the day at his bar in Hollywood called The Hub." For six intense weeks, a committed group of ten to fifteen gay men talked, planned, and organized a two-pronged strategy of resistance—in the street and in the courtroom.

"What's important about the Black Cat from a legal perspective," says attorney David Farah, Alexei's life partner, "is that the gay men fought the case not on the basis of entrapment, but on the legal theory that they had equal rights and did nothing to be arrested for. That was a tremendous mind-set change. It's one of those moments in gay history where things changed dramatically. It was a quantum leap." To fight the legal case, defendants turned to the Tavern Guild, an association of gay bar owners who came together to support gay rights causes. Large jars bearing the sign Tavern Guild Legal Aid Fund were placed in hundreds of gay bars throughout L.A. and San Francisco. (It is estimated that there were over 100 gay bars in L.A. alone.)

At the same time, organizers planned a demonstration in front of the Black Cat bar. "We didn't want a tiny protest of fifteen or twenty people," says Alexei. "That had been done before. We wanted as many people out as possible. But we were scared. We were terrified that if we were photographed at the rally we would lose our jobs, our incomes, our families. And there was also the fear of being beaten up by the police. A few months earlier, hippies had protested on the Sunset Strip and the kids were attacked and beaten by the sheriff and the police. We knew it could happen to us." Indeed, L.A. in the early '60s had become a hotbed of violence between police and the public. It wasn't just the gay community that bore the brunt of police batons.

ON weekend nights, the Strip was jammed with teenagers. Some local business owners were put off by the flower children who clogged the sidewalks but spent little money. Under pressure from these property owners, the police started to harass, arrest, and haul away the "loitering" teens. In response, Al Mitchell formed RAMCOM—the Right of Assembly and Movement Committee. RAMCOM organized a series of protests that turned into violent clashes between long-haired youths and heavily armed riot police. The Sunset Strip "massacres" were immortalized in the Buffalo Springfield anthem "For What It's Worth" and the low-budget movie *Riot on Sunset Strip*.

As police harassment continued, RAMCOM next planned six simultaneous demonstrations against "police lawlessness." The demonstrations would take place on Saturday night, February 11, 1967—in Watts, Pacoima, East Los Angeles, Sunset Strip, Venice, and Silverlake. The Silverlake demonstration was organized in conjunction with the gay Black Cat organizers. Eighty thousand flyers announcing the rallies made their way into clubs, bars, coffeehouses, college campuses, and high schools throughout the city.

The Free Press reported that "One of the most interesting and pace-setting reactions to the call to demonstrate came early this week from homosexual organizers who are currently up in arms about New Year's Eve police raids in a number of Silverlake area

Demonstrators at the Black Cat on Feb. 11, 1967

gay bars. ... Members of such homophile groups as pride and the Council on Religion and the Homosexual decided to sponsor the sixth demonstration to protest the bar raids and resulting beatings and brutality." In a precedent-setting achievement, gays and straights joined forces to fight against the police violence that affected so many communities throughout the city. But the united front hit some bumps. A prime example: gay activists bowed to pressure from straight organizers, agreeing to omit the word "homosexual" from their flyers.

Meetings, phone calls, flyers, lawyers, court dates, and more phone calls later, the big day arrived. On February 11th, 3,000 people marched down the Sunset Strip carrying signs saying things like "Stop Blue Fascism" and "Free the Strip." Starting at Pandora's Box, wave after wave of teenagers, flower children, college students, and adults paraded down the Strip in a spirited but peaceful protest.

Most of the other demonstrations flopped, however. In Venice, only about twenty protesters showed up. In Pacoima, a tiny group of teen activists was attacked by local gang members, who beat up the kids and ripped up their signs as police watched without interfering. In Watts and East L.A., protests failed to occur at all (perhaps due to the organizers' lack of connection to the black and brown communities).

The Silverlake rally, however, was a huge success. About 500 protesters gathered outside the Black Cat. The crowd was so large that it spilled out from the sidewalk, filling an adjacent parking lot. Picketers carried signs reading "Abolish Arbitrary Arrests" and "No More Abuse of our Rights and Dignity." Religious leaders, attorneys, and gay activists addressed the crowd over loudspeakers from the parking lot. Police monitored the scene at the Black Cat from across the street but kept their distance. Protesters passed out leaflets to passing drivers explaining what the demonstration was all about. Some motorists beeped their horns in support of the demonstrators. Others shouted obscenities as they drove by.

"I was terrified," remembers Alexei. "I was thinking that someone could drive by and shoot me. So there was fear, but also a sense of pride. We weren't hiding anymore. I was standing out in front of the public, being myself, saying 'This is who I am. I deserve the same rights as everybody else. I deserve not to be beat, not to be arrested just for being me.'"

Despite its historical significance as the largest gay protest to date, the Black Cat demonstration was ignored by the mainstream press. However the Free Press covered the rally extensively, declaring: "The Los Angeles homosexual community—long reluctant to come out into the open—now appears ready to launch an entirely new kind of civil rights drive. A drive demanding equal treatment for sexual minorities."

While it didn't make the splash that the Stonewall riots did two years later, the Black Cat resistance marked a turning point in gay history. Asserting in court that gays deserve equal protection under the law set legal precedent. The fledgling pride newsletter morphed into *The Advocate*—the largest and most influential publication in the history of the gay press. Even the naming of the gay pride movement, and the deeply meaningful use of the word "pride" when referring to gay liberation and new gay consciousness, was born with Steve Ginsberg's PRIDE organization, whose first political action was the protest at the Black Cat.

On November 7, 2008, the Black Cat Tavern was declared a Los Angeles Historic-Cultural Monument. Now home to a Latino gay bar named El Barcito, the building still sports the original sign depicting a smiling black and white cat. Says Alexei: "The fight for civil rights in American happened in many places: at Gettysburg, at Selma and Montgomery, Alabama—these are physical places where people can go and say, 'This is where black civil rights started.' The Black Cat protest is our Gettysburg. It's our Selma. It's where gay men and women can go and learn about our history. This is where the first large demonstration of gay people in the nation, maybe the world, happened. It happened right here in Los Angeles."

How the Castro Became 'The Castro'

TIMOTHY STEWART-WINTER

SAN Francisco's Castro District was the first big-city neighborhood in the U.S. where openly gay people elected one of their own to represent them in City Hall. Harvey Milk, the man who was elected in this capacity in 1977, soon became nationally prominent as the leading spokesperson for gay and lesbian rights in a bitterly fought contest over a 1978 statewide ballot measure that would have banned homosexuals from serving as schoolteachers. The Castro's mythical status was cemented by the assassination of Milk and Mayor George Moscone less than a year into Milk's first term, and by the so-called White Night Riots that followed the lenient sentence given to Dan White, the former police officer who murdered them. Today the Castro's terrain of hilly asphalt is a site of pilgrimage, its bars and restaurants home to a lucrative tourist trade and a gay nightlife scene.

But how did the Castro come to be the world's most famous gay neighborhood in the first place? Most accounts focus on two processes. First, gay artists, hippies, and radicals migrated to central San Francisco during and after the 1967 "Summer of Love" in the Haight-Ashbury district, which is nearly adjacent to the Castro. These adventuresome urban pioneers are said to have "discovered" the hidden charm of the picturesque Victorian houses that had suffered long years of neglect under a regimen of asbestos, tar paper, and aluminum siding perpetrated by clueless heterosexuals. The second narrative centers on the mobilization of gay activists, including Milk, who demanded and won the right to be open about their homosexuality and obtain political representation.

Both narratives throw the spotlight on the people who built the Castro district rather than on the larger social conditions in which they operated. In point of fact, the "gayification" of the Castro was strongly affected by the processes of urban change and political development that were taking place at this time.

Between 1849 and 1915, real estate developers built nearly 50,000 Victorian houses in San Francisco. One of the major developers claimed that his goal was to "transform the sandy wastes outside the business part of the city into ... neighborhoods, composed of frugal and industrious people," asserting that their great aspiration was to "serve the great middle class" of the young city, declared Anne Bloomfield in the March 1978 *Journal of the Society of Architectural Historians*.

The area around the Castro Street commercial strip was just far enough from San Francisco's northeastern core that its Victorian houses escaped destruction in the 1906 earthquake and fire. This area, long known as Eureka Valley, or sometimes by the name of Most Holy Redeemer Parish, was populated by white ethnics, mostly Catholics, from the 1920s—when the Twin Peaks tunnel brought increased traffic to the area—to the early 70s. Nestled in a valley, unencumbered by tenements or high-rises, Eureka Valley in the 40s and 50s seemed to its residents to be almost self-contained. It was home to small business owners, church officials, schoolteachers, professionals, club organizers, and above all skilled, unionized workers in the waterfront industries of one of America's busiest ports. The city's gay and lesbian community institutions—its bars—were elsewhere, in the city's dense northeastern quadrant near the waterfront. The Castro Theatre, built in 1924, was only one of several movie palaces in the neighborhood, but it was the sole one to survive the invention of television.

Having sifted through the historical record on the Castro, I concluded that the dense concentration of storefront taverns along the two or three blocks of Castro Street just below Market was at least as crucial a factor in its gayification as the Victorian houses. Bars had long been central cultural institutions for white men in America's immigrant centers, and San Francisco, known as the "wettest in the West," resisted federal and state enforcement of Prohibition.

The elderly men and women that filmmaker Peter Stein interviewed for his documentary *The Castro* (KQED television, 1997) recall that the two-block commercial strip on Castro Street alone had nine bars in the post-World War II period. "The consumption of alcohol on a Saturday night per capita was tremendous," one man recalled. Liquor licenses were difficult and expensive to obtain, and when commercial properties changed hands in San Francisco, the licenses frequently remained in place, constituting a neglected feature of the Castro's built environment. In 1950, men made up the majority of Eureka Valley's employed adults, and among them, the largest fraction (46 percent) worked in traditionally blue-collar occupations on the city's waterfront or in the skilled trades. Thirty percent of employed men and 66 percent of employed women worked in non-managerial clerical, sales, or service positions.

But the neighborhood's economic foundation was beginning to deteriorate. Blue-collar jobs, homes, and families all began to leave San Francisco, replaced by white-collar office jobs in the newly built downtown skyscrapers. As shipping was automated and moved across the Bay to Oakland, so too did the waterfront jobs that Eureka Valley men had long held. In the 1950s, the city's banking employment nearly doubled, but maritime employment dropped by a quarter; the white population dropped thirteen percent while the black population increased 43 percent. National trends hurt San Francisco's traditional industries, including timber, oil, and food processing, and companies also sought to escape the city's powerful unions.

By the 1960s, white blue-collar family men were increasingly moving to the suburbs, and the city's adult population was growing younger, more white-collar, and more professional. Spending several nights a week drinking in taverns was not this crowd's idea of a good time. The decline of the male-dominated, "family wage" economy of Eureka Valley was becoming untenable, and women and gay men were challenging longstanding norms. Above all, unlike their straight brothers, San Francisco's growing gay minority patronized the bars faithfully. In 1969, gay liberationist Carl Wittman declared that "San Francisco is a refugee camp for homosexuals"—and this would only become more true in the following decade.

THE gay men and women who first made the Castro a gay neighborhood were hippies and other dropouts from middle-class America. In crucial respects, they were as much dissenters from American mass consumer culture as they were its vanguard. Geographers Mickey Lauria and Lawrence Knopp noted in 1985 (in *Urban Geography* 6) that "relatively low-wage gay renters seeking nothing more than a place to live are sometimes the catalysts in a central-city neighborhood's upgrading." They added that eventually this "first wave ... may attract other more affluent gays to the neighborhood, especially if it is ripe for redevelopment." Many, including Harvey Milk, were themselves displaced by sharp rent increases during the gentrification process.

Gay people were moving into the Castro in the '60s because it was cheap. According to a group of urban studies scholars associated with geographer Neil Smith, a professor at the City University of New York, gentrification occurs when there's a gap between an area's "actual ground rent" and "potential ground rent." Deindustrialization and white flight had deflated the value of Eureka Valley's Victorians, pushing prices down.

In 1963, the Missouri Mule opened on Market Street near Castro, becoming the first bar in Eureka Valley to attract a predominantly gay clientele. Like most gay bars at the time, it was small and poorly lit, its windows painted over so people on the street couldn't see inside. For David Valentine, a printer I interviewed, the presence of the Missouri Mule made Eureka Valley attractive after he quit *The San Francisco Examiner*, where he'd had to conceal his homosexuality carefully. He wanted to open his own print shop. "One of the reasons I had located my business up here was there was a gay bar across the street," he recalled. Valentine rented a cheap, run-down flat on Market Street in 1968. "When I moved in there I was on an army cot in a sleeping bag, and worked on it for the better part of the year," he said, "all the way up to putting finish on the floor and staining them a dark walnut and then recoating them with polyurethane."

The gayification of the Castro was a transition from one masculine tavern subculture to another. The late Allan Bérubé, a gay man who was living in a Haight-Ashbury commune at this time (and author of the acclaimed 1990 book *Coming Out Under Fire: The History of Gay Men and Women in World War II*), recalled walking downhill into the Castro in search of bars that would tolerate groups of gay patrons. The process of succession in taverns was gradual. One bar even turned gay and then turned back, acquiring a straight clientele once again: "The Mistake on 18th near Castro is now straight and has a new name," wrote a columnist in *California Scene*, a gay nightlife magazine, in 1971. "When a butch but older character there asked me if I knew the latest ball scores, I knew something was wrong."

Gay hippies created communal living arrangements markedly different from those of the straight nuclear families around them. Newly arrived migrants moved in with friends from back home in the American heartland, in a process that closely resembled classic ethnic patterns of chain migration. Newcomers participated in an alternative economic and social support system, separated not only from the patterns of postwar nuclear family life but also from the regimen of government subsidies, mortgages, and bank loans on which the latter depended. Although its gay population was and is male dominated, lesbians gravitated there as well.

A key part of the Castro's history, discussed at some length in the Shilts biography, is the extent to which some Eureka Valley heterosexuals resisted the arrival of visibly gay people and businesses in the early '70s. As Berkeley sociologist Manuel Castells noted in *The City and the Grassroots* (1983): "Gay settlement was opposed by property, family, and high class: the old triumvirate of social conservatism." Straight residents fought back against the gay onslaught using strategies familiar to many urbanites, including that most tried-and-true tactic, violence, which took the form of gay-bashing and vandalism. They also used the apparatus of municipal government to curtail or criminalize "undesirable" ways of using the neighborhood, such as cruising. And an exclusive neighborhood association of business owners, the Eureka Valley Merchants Association, conspired to out gay business owners.

In the crucial summer of 1971, three or four area gay bars mushroomed to seven or eight. On Memorial Day weekend, Toad Hall opened, a bar that became a hit with gay men from all over San Francisco. The Muni Metro subway line under Market Street would soon make the area even more accessible. In May 1971, *The San Francisco Examiner* ran a profile of Eureka Valley, noting that it "is experiencing a big influx of very young and very hip people. Many 'street artists' have 'discovered' Eureka Valley and as a result the Castro and Market area has some of the best head, arts and crafts shops and galleries around." Six weeks later, the *Chronicle* asked, "Will Eureka Valley become a new Haight-Ashbury?" and concluded, "Old-time residents undoubtedly hope not."

Leafing through neighborhood newspapers from the period shows that two radically different populations were living near Castro Street. In the *Noe Eureka Weekly Shopper*, whose complete run from June 1971 to March 1972 is preserved in the San Francisco History Room in the downtown public library, you can glimpse the lives of older, longtime residents drawn together by bingo nights, parish musicals, and clubs celebrating shared Irish, Italian, or Scandinavian descent. In the summer of 1971, articles debated the opening of "new and unusual stores" and expressed "the feeling of seeing the city or the neighborhood seemingly taken over by outsiders."

In contrast, *The Castro Village Other*, available in the GLBT Historical Society, preserves the lives of gays, hippies, and radicals. In the summer of 1972, one young man advertised for a roommate who was "into bio-degradable detergents [and] into the spiritual trip." Another wrote, "young and interesting Nordic-American male age 27, seeks friends, male or female for tripping and fun." By August, a gay columnist wrote in *California Scene* that around Castro Street, "local residents have gotten uptight, the police are beginning to drop by the [gay] bars and roving gangs of youths (possibly taking their cue from their parents) are beating up gay guys on their way home at night."

Gays and lesbians began to organize a response to this harassment. At a September 7, 1971, community meeting to elect a new chair for the Eureka Valley Police–Community Relations Council, the fifteen or so "straights" who showed up were dismayed to find some 300 gay men in attendance. One of two anti-gay candidates for the position, a California highway patrolman and president of the Most Holy Redeemer Parent–Teachers' Guild, declared he was "fed up with all the hand-holding in the streets. My wife and child can't go outside without being scandalized." The lopsided turnout meant the two anti-gay candidates and their supporters walked out frustrated. The gay constituency elected their own candidate, a straight former policeman named Bob Pettengill who owned a Castro Street restaurant with a predominantly gay clientele. The *Chronicle* declared: "A Gay Victory in Eureka Valley." The next month, a front-page article said, "San Francisco's populous homosexual community, historically non-political and inward looking, is in the midst of assembling a potentially powerful political machine."

For the next three years, tensions were fairly high. Toad Hall and other gay bars were repeatedly damaged in suspicious fires. In July 1973, the home of the pioneering gay Metropolitan Community Church (MCC) burned to the ground. Police continued to arrest gay men for dancing in bars and clubs and cruising in parks. By 1974, the Gay Activist Alliance had recorded sixty beatings of gays citywide in a three-month period, with the Castro having the worst record of all.

In late summer 1974, neighborhood resentments came to a head. Late at night on Labor Day, after the bars had closed, fourteen men were arrested in what the *Chronicle* called "a sweep to clear the Castro Street sidewalks." They were charged with public drunkenness, obstructing traffic, resisting arrest, disturbing the peace, and drug offenses. Harvey Milk, who had lost his first bid for supervisor the previous year, rallied others to defend the so-called "Castro 14," charging that they were arrested solely because they were gay. A straight woman wrote to the *Chronicle* in defense of the police sweep: "The smell of pot almost knocks you out as you edge by. They have completely taken over Castro Street and I'm made to feel like an intruder in their own little world—me, a native of the district. They walk around in torn jeans with their private parts showing." But before long, all charges were dropped. According to Shilts, this "sealed the neighborhood's reputation as the new homosexual hot spot."

Meanwhile, gay people opening businesses in the neighborhood found that the Eureka Valley Merchants Association (EVMA), in the words of printer David Valentine, "didn't want to have anything to do with us." In 1970 or 1971, when the EVMA refused to admit Ian Ingham, an antique store owner, he founded the Castro Village Association (CVA), made up largely of gay and hippie businesses. Even a relatively conservative gay shop owner complained in print about "the rigidly anti-gay, deeply Catholic Merchants Association." In the Shilts biography, the conflict between the two business groups is depicted as a pitched battle. My research hints, however, that it may have been somewhat more fluid. Indeed, in December 1971, the CVA placed a front-page notice in the *Weekly Shopper* thanking the EVMA for its "unexpected, surprise and most welcome, substantial contribution" to promoting the CVA's Christmas events. The following month, the same paper—the paper of the old-timers—even profiled Ingham as "merchant of the week." In time, the Castro Village Association won out over EVMA. And "Castro Village," a branding effort promoted beginning in 1974 by the CVA, became the most common way of referring to the neighborhood, gradually morphing into "the Castro."

PART III

Flash Forward: Aftermath and Diffusion

After Stonewall: Liberation and Libido

ANDREW HOLLERAN

THE first thing that struck me about these essays on the 1970s that you're about to read is that they're for the most part about the *early* years of that decade—the first gay pride marches in New York and Los Angeles, for instance, took place in 1970—though reading the memoirs by Karla Jay and Ellen Shumsky describing attempts to form gay political organizations, one is struck by how "Sixties" they all were: the abhorrence of authority, the consciousness-raising, the aversion to organizational hierarchy. Even in the photographs of the first gay pride march in Steven Dansky's essay, "The Look of Gay Liberation," it's still all about '60s hair, '60s clothes, and the '60s counterculture. And, confirming the adage that a picture is worth a thousand words, the ebullience evident in Peter Hujar's photo of the first marchers reminds us that gay liberation came out of the same impulse as the Summer of Love (1967).

It's painful to see those faces now—not only because everyone was so young, but because it's a reminder of how those ideals of community, of Walt Whitman's adhesiveness, were swamped by the tsunami of promiscuity that soon deluged cities like New York City, San Francisco, and Los Angeles, the very cities in which the parades were held. By 1976, communitarian ideals had surrendered to the fact that there were "So Many Men, So Little Time"; though by the beginning of the 1980s and the onslaught of AIDS, that song had acquired a grim new meaning, since there was no time at all for many of those marchers.

When I first got to New York, I was told to go to dances at the

Firehouse—a '60s venue where politics were as important as sex—but I went only once because it all seemed, well, so '60s. I was more interested in what would become the '70s: the bars and baths, the Fire Island so well described in Felice Picano's essay. And that seems to me now the irony of gay liberation. Although the pride marches got bigger every year, by 1975 many of my friends preferred to stay at the beach than come into town to participate. Indeed, gay politics was not the real story of this decade. Nor was it the relationship between lesbians and gay men. These essays—four by women, three by men—only remind us that there never was much common ground between gay men and lesbians, until caretaking and ACT UP brought them together. I had no female friends during that decade; I was too absorbed in the bars, the baths, and the beach. The '70s were all about coming out, as Steven F. Dansky, marching with a group called Flaming Faggots, notes; but it was AIDS that ended up advancing gay rights more than anything else.

As for my piece—an excerpt from a talk I gave to a gay group at Harvard in 1992—the question I asked that evening still resonates in my mind. One night I was walking down Christopher Street with a college classmate who'd moved to Paris after graduation, settled down with another man, and started what turned out to be a very successful business—in other words, one of those people who knew what he wanted long before the rest of us did. At one point we passed a kiosk selling the gay male porn magazines that flourished in the late '70s. After surveying them for a moment, my friend asked why, as he put it, did Americans make so much of homosexuality?

I didn't know what to say at the time, but years later, reading these essays, it seems inevitable that Americans would make much of it. In the land of freedom, individuality, and the pursuit of happiness, how could they not? Gay liberation was like that exhilarating high note that Jewelle Gomez describes in her memories of the singer Sylvester: the life force itself. Gay liberation was an upwelling of energy produced by winning the Second World War, getting rich, and finding ourselves far from our Victorian forefathers, a logical expansion of civil rights.

Today gay men and lesbians still exist in mostly separate universes, but we have gay marriage, gay parents, gay politicians, gay sitcoms, and gay soldiers—such conventional roles compared to the radical lesbianism of the '70s zeitgeist! And the parade that was so radical and brave in 1970 has now become a sort of carnival with corporate sponsors attended by large numbers of straight people. But that, I guess, is the genius of American life—its capacity to assimilate—which is where we are now: assimilation and its discontents. The '70s were probably the last time in which gay people thought they might create new forms of adhesiveness.

October 2018

Figure 1. Fred W. McDarrah's photograph outside the Stonewall Inn on June 27, 1969. In Gay Pride: Photographs from Stonewall to Today *(1994), by Fred W. McDarrah and Timothy S. McDarrah.*

Figure 2. Ellen Shumsky, "Gail Russo and Diana Davies, GFL Gay-In, Central Park, N.Y.C., May 1970." Reprinted with permission.

The Look of Gay Liberation

STEVEN F. DANSKY

THE early photographers of lesbian and gay liberation confronted ambiguity by shooting photographs of out-in-the-open GLBT people, images of unequivocal candidness. Forty years ago, dating from the Stonewall Rebellion in 1969, it was daring and risky to be the subject of a photograph depicting gay liberation, unabashed and full-framed, the physical declaration of political and sexual identity. Unlike the coded photographs of earlier generations, the ones of the early Gay Liberation era were taken with breathtaking directness. These images serve as a permanent record of the life-affirming sexual identities that emerged during that era.

In *On Photography*, Susan Sontag observed that photographs have intrinsic value as social commentary and that "social change is replaced by a change in images." The story of GLBT people needed to be told. The subjects in images had to be accessible, real, and vulnerable if they were to be effective. In order for social change to occur, there has to be evidence of the event, as in the photograph by Fred W. McDarrah for *The Village Voice* of the Stonewall Rebellion (Figure 1). The intimate photographs of Ellen Shumsky are a perfect example of this. Despite being taken in the public square of Central Park's Sheep Meadow surrounded by tens of thousands at New York's first gay pride march in 1970, the lesbian subjects in Shumsky's image appear to share a private moment (Figure 2). And in the documentary photograph by Diana Davies, an image also of the first march that portrays the exultation of social progress (Figure 3).

ANATOMY OF A PHOTOGRAPH

Peter Hujar (1934–1987) was one of the most important American photographers of the late 20th century, having influenced Nan

Figure 3. Diana Davies. "Gay 'Be-In,' Sheep Meadow, Central Park, New York, June 28, 1970." Reprinted with permission of Diana Davies Photographs, Manuscripts and Archives Division, New York Public Library.

Goldin and Robert Mapplethorpe, among others. Hujar photographed drag queens, gay cruisers, corporate high-rises, dilapidated diners, crumbling Newark apartments, and animals. He's probably best known for his portraits, some of which are in the permanent collection of New York's Metropolitan Museum of Art.

Before Hujar withdrew from fashion photography in the 1970's, he took a photograph that is generically titled "Gay Liberation Poster Image," which I prefer to call the "Come Out!" photograph after the poster that made it famous (Figures 4). Annie Leibovitz wrote in *Annie Leibovitz: at Work*: "Some pictures attain resonance as documents of their time." The "Come Out!" photo is such an image. Its meaning has been variously interpreted, but its original use was as a poster for the Gay Liberation Front (GLF), New York, with the overlay text, "Come Out!! Join the Sisters and Brothers of the Gay Liberation Front." The poster from its conception was meant to be printed in large numbers. GLF member Judy Reif remembers wallpapering the GLF poster on the sides of buildings in Greenwich Village: "The poster was going to recruit people for the first gay pride march in June 1970." To my knowledge, the Hujar photograph was never exhibited or published at that time as an image distinct from the poster.

It is the most iconic photograph of Gay Liberation; no image better captures the spirit of the first year after the Stonewall Rebellion. The image seems cinematographic, an encapsulated frame or a film still, completely uncompromising—which is why it worked as a political poster. In *Outlaw Representation: Censorship and Homosexuality in Twentieth-Century American Art*, art historian Richard Meyer said of the "Come Out!" photograph: "It stages gay liberation as a utopian space beyond the reaches of State power and social control."

It was on an early Sunday morning in the Flatiron District—usually a pulsating and congested Manhattan square that was silent and motionless at that hour—that eighteen members of GLF waited at a street corner on Fifth Avenue. The enigmatic, soft-spoken Hujar arrived with five-o'clock shadow, carrying a camera. He

Figure 4. Photo: © Peter Hujar. "Gay Liberation Poster Image," 1970. Gelatin-silver print. Reprinted with permission of The Peter Hujar Archive, Courtesy Matthew Marks Gallery, NY.

climbed the pedestal of a lamppost, balanced himself, and directed his subjects as if choreographing a show. His subjects ran down the street away from him. "Run toward me," he called. From that somewhat elevated angle with the camera focused on his huddled subjects, he shot the image at just the right moment.

Although several subjects in the photograph have placed its location elsewhere, Hujar shot the photograph at 19th Street between Fifth Avenue and the Avenue of the Americas. The site was a few blocks away from Hujar's commercial studio on West 23rd Street, which he operated from 1969 to 1970.

Martin Duberman described Hujar's staging of the photograph, which he used for the cover of his 1993 book, *Stonewall*, in this way: "In the final poster, the fifteen marchers crowd the center, and it only gradually becomes clear that the sidewalks behind them are empty; these ebullient troops seem to have no backup forces." The photograph has power and energy through Hujar's use of linear perspective, with the street from Fifth Avenue to the Avenue of the Americas becoming the vanishing point. Most subjects of the early photographs of Gay Liberation, while out enough to be photographed, were not named in any caption and are thus anonymous. However, I was able to identify a number of the people in the "Come Out!" photograph, and even tracked down a number to get their recollections about the photo shoot.

The mood of the photograph is unambiguously euphoric. Hujar's lens captured a fractional image, as all photographs must be. The photographer chooses what's inside and outside the frame. There were hidden subjects invisible to the lens and absent from the shoot. Indeed the decision to come out and appear in the photograph was an intense struggle for many who showed up. New York City public school teacher Ron Ballard, dually oppressed as gay and African-American, told a fellow GLFer that he just couldn't do the photograph and always regretted it. He feared recrimination as a teacher. Nearly 25 years later, however, Ballard appeared in PBS' *Out Rage, '69*, by filmmaker Arthur Dong, a documentary about the gay and lesbian liberation movement.

Out of the Closet

The first Gay Pride march, in 1970, was all about coming out of the closet, and tens of thousands of people did. It was announced on simple white cardstock with deliberate gay panache and the message: "You are invited to Gay Liberation's First Birthday Celebration ... Sunday, June 28, 1970 ... Mass March up Sixth Avenue to Central Park's Sheep Meadow for Gay-In. Assemble at Sheridan Square, 12–1 PM."

I marched with the Flaming Faggots, a group that I started with Kenneth Pitchford, with whom I later cofounded the New York Effeminists. Along with the other group members—Joseph Canarelli, Michael Danchese, Robert Miller, and Michael O'Hara—we advanced, shoulder to shoulder, from Christopher Street to the Avenue of the Americas, turning northward at Milligan Place and 10th Street, where several photographs were taken of us. One shot by Pulitzer Prize-nominated Michael Evans was published *The New York Times*, showing only the backs of our heads. Two other photographs were taken by Fred McDarrah, renowned Beat-generation chronicler, at the exact same location and published in *The Village Voice*. In one photograph, there are only back of heads as in the Evans image. But surprisingly, McDarrah shot a second photograph, the flipside of first, revealing the faces of the subjects (Figure 5).

It is the rare photograph that conveys the private circumstances under which individuals process change. Ellen Shumsky revealed claustrophobic intimacy in a very personal moment of group political contemplation in her photograph of a Radicalesbian meeting (Figure 6). Each woman listens attentively to a

Figure 5. At the first Gay Pride march in New York, June 28, 1970. Photo by Fred W. McDarrah for The Village Voice *appeared in* In Gay Pride: Photographs from Stonewall to Today.

Figure 6. Ellen Shumsky, "Radicalesbians Committee Meeting," 1970. Reprinted with permission.

speaker who gestures with an outstretched hand like an appeal. Shumsky, an early member of GLF, a founding member of Radicalesbians, and one of the authors of *The Woman-Identified Woman*, commented on the photograph—possibly taken at Rita Mae Brown's East 15th Street apartment as noted by one subject in the photograph (though not verified by Shumsky): "It was a meeting of Radicalesbians on Manhattan's Lower East Side. I remember every woman in the photograph. I don't recall what the meeting was about, but I know it wasn't a consciousness-raising group meeting or a meeting for the writing of 'The Woman-Identified Woman.' It must have been about some group or political issue."

The photograph of the signing of "The Effeminist Manifesto" (from left: Kenneth Pitchford, this writer, and John Knoebel) seems like a vignette, lacking sharpness, but the image successfully evokes a sense of the clandestine (Figure 7). The "Manifesto" was a germinal work of queer theory that has been anthologized several times. In *American So-*

Figure 7. Signing the Effeminist Manifesto, 1973. Polaroid by Robin Morgan. Used with permission.

cial Movements: Gay Rights Movement, Jennifer Smith described it as "one of the most enduring documents to emerge from the modern gay liberation movement."

Other photographs of gay liberation are important in order to establish the intense activism of the early movement, such as the Times Square protest against police harassment that degenerated into what became known as "The August 1970 Riot" (Figure 8). The event was reported in *The New York Times* (8/30/70) as follows: "Several hundred youths roamed through Greenwich Village last night and early this morning after a demonstration by homosexual organizations ended." John Knoebel, an early gay activist and GLF member, recalled: "'Join Us! Join us!' rang out. For what, to do what? Who knew? But the surge was unstoppable. It was a hot night in the Village. Hundreds of people just started shouting. 'Gay Power! Gay Power Now!' The march was fully overwhelmed by the size of the crowd and ceased to exist. And this was the moment when the march became the riot. All pandemonium let loose. Sirens started howling as squad cars arrived and police tried to clear the streets."

Figure 8. "Gay Liberation Front marches on Times Square, New York City," 1970. Diana Davies photo. Reprinted with permission of Diana Davies Photographs, The New York Public Library.

The Radicalesbians

ELLEN SHUMSKY

AUTHOR'S NOTE: The first half of this article was originally published in 1970 in the broadsheet ComeOut! *The second half was to have been published in a 1972 issue of* ComeOut! *Some time before production, the print shop that housed the galleys was raided (perpetrators unknown—at least to me) and the galleys were destroyed. The latter half of this article, tracing the rise and fall of Radicalesbians, never made it to press.*

RADICALESBIANS began during the dreary months of the dying winter of 1970. A nucleus of Gay Liberation Front women, with a growing women's consciousness, began to feel the need for an all-women's GLF dance. They had previously been working on and attending GLF dances, which were overwhelmingly attended by males. The oppressive atmosphere was a simulated gay men's bar—an overcrowded, dimly lit room where most human contact was limited to groping and dry fucking, packed together subway rush-hour style.

Earlier attempts by women and some men to create an ambience that encouraged group dancing and space for conversation were nullified by the "pack-'em-in" attitude of the GLF men running the dances. There were so many men at each event that the women felt lost to each other. It was intolerable to many, but the women put up with it, hoping it would change. Finally when it became obvious it was only growing worse as the weather grew warmer, GLF women decided to have an all-women's dance.

This first dance was a great success: an environment of women—rapping, drinking, dancing, relating with fluidity and grace—was a new and beautiful phenomenon. That dance was followed by several more. Besides enjoying the events, the women had to meet and work together. Weekly meetings of GLF women became routine. This provided a fine opportunity to work collectively and to get to know one another. At the same time, something else was happening. Some GLF women, together with feminists from the Women's Liberation Movement, had formed a consciousness-raising group. Out of these meetings two major accomplishments materialized: the writing of the lesbian feminist manifesto, "The Woman Identified Woman"; and a plan to confront the issue of lesbianism at the National Organization for Women (NOW)'s 2nd Congress to Unite Women.

At the Congress, held on May 1, 1970, twenty women wearing lavender T-shirts stenciled with "lavender menace" liberated the microphone from the line-up of planned speakers and initiated a forum on why lesbianism was the most threatening and most avoided issue in the Women's Movement. The entire audience of 400 women related to the topic of lesbianism through their own personal experiences and feelings. This was followed by two days of workshops attended by more than 200 women. The paper "The Woman Identified Woman" was distributed. Our resolutions became part of the report of the conference: "Women's liberation is a lesbian plot. We are all lesbian." Instead of purging lesbians from the Women's Movement, we will proudly own and assert the woman-identified woman in all of us.

The aftermath of the congress coup is not so well known. We called for consciousness–raising groups, and fifty interested women met the call. Four groups were set up, with new women from the NOW Congress and Lavender Menace lesbians participating in each group. Many of the women in these groups were straight-identified women who wanted to confront the issue of lesbianism and perhaps the lesbian in themselves. A very large majority turned out to be active lesbians, latent lesbians, closeted lesbians, one-beautiful-experience lesbians, freaked-out lesbians, spaced-out lesbians. From the ranks of the Women's Liberation Movement they responded.

After having related for months and years to the broader women's issues at the sacrifice of their own sexual identities, these women were ready now to come out—to use their energies to create a lesbian community and to make sure that the concepts of primary value and commitment between women, developed in the paper "Woman Identified Woman," were taken on by the Women's Liberation Movement. These sisters started coming to our weekly GLF women's meetings, and as word spread through the grapevine, more and more unaffiliated women started attending those meetings.

At that point, the various groups of women had so thoroughly merged that the name GLF Women seemed inappropriate. It was obvious we were an independent, autonomous group, and while there were some women who continued to relate to GLF, there were many feminists who felt they could not affiliate with a male-dominated organization that was in large part sexist. We decided to drop the name GLF Women and create a treasury to relate to our own needs and the needs of other gay women. The money was taken from the GLF community center fund—that portion that had been contributed by the women who had been attending GLF dances. It was enough to fund our first independent dance under our new name, "Radicalesbians."

In this way, a movement of radical and revolutionary gay women organically coalesced—not artificially out of some theoretical political necessity, but through the natural flow of our experiences and changes in consciousness. Difficulties were anticipated because priorities differed. Some women felt themselves to be an arm of the Women's Liberation Movement. They viewed the struggle as one waged by women against male supremacy. They experienced their primary identity as women (with a difference). Others felt themselves to be in close affiliation with GLF; they continued to relate to GLF and viewed the struggle as one primarily between heterosexuals and homosexuals. Still others saw their situation as unique—a struggle against sexism through the prism of a gay woman's consciousness. Some women had not shaped or articulated their politics. They only knew that they liked to be with their sisters and wanted to help. With these differences we began meeting and working together, respecting if not loving each other.

BECAUSE of our past experiences in the GLF and other movement groups, we came together committed to finding an organizational form that would avoid the pitfalls of entrenched leadership hierarchies. We did not want a situation in which a few leaders represented and ran an organization in the interests of an apathetic community and ultimately in their own self-interest, as their community abandoned a boring, non-growth situation. A marathon weekend was planned, during which randomly arranged small groups of women talked about the issues they felt a gay women's organization should address. The fifty or so topics that emerged from this marathon weekend were written up on poster boards that became our scrolls. These were ceremonially unrolled at meetings each week and became known as our "agenda." In the course of discussing each item on the agenda, we hoped that the shape of our organization would emerge. It was not to be predefined but would assume the shape of our collective needs.

Immediately adopted was the lot system for randomly selecting women to write up minutes, speak at colleges, and attend to the variety of tasks that are ordinarily dealt with by an election or a volunteer system. The lot system ideally would involve every woman in all the tasks of the organization and protect the group from domination by strong women with better-developed skills to the detriment of everyone else's growth. Our discussions followed the procedure of each woman who spoke calling on the next woman to her left who wished to speak. Thus we avoided a chairwoman and the kinds of manipulation that are possible when one person becomes the center of an organizational universe.

However, in spite of all our efforts to keep a leadership syndrome from establishing itself, it became clear that one was emerging. Women with organizational experience and clearly articulated political ideas tended to dominate the discussions. They had the most to say and spoke every time during the circle reached them. They became vortices around which other women's vague, ill-defined, or scarcely felt political inclinations flowed. And while their ideas were needed, women grew to resent them because it was felt that somehow they were responsible for this failing attempt at a truly participatory forum.

When some of the most committed and articulate women decided to leave New York and stopped coming to the meetings, it became clear how much of the group energy had centered on their seeming political clarity. Their organizational experience, well-developed feminist consciousness, commitment, and dedication to the necessity of constructing a viable large-group political forum had fed and directed the group. In their absence, the group floundered.

For a while, one woman, clearly committed to large group politics, functioned as an unacknowledged leader, but that caused conflict with the basic premise of the necessity for a non-hierarchical form. A fundamental contradiction in the situation was brought into sharp focus. On one level, the group took responsibility and understood that a leader was created and indulged out of fears and weakness. On another level, it was felt that this situation inhibited our growth and kept us locked into old oppressive forms.

Instead of dealing with these contradictions, the group began to direct its frustration and resentment at its most visible target—the leader. During this time, attendance at the meetings began to decline rapidly. Perhaps some women were disgusted by what seemed like obvious hypocrisy. Perhaps they were disappointed and not committed enough to the struggle. Perhaps they simply did not know what to do. But the fact was that numbers and energy were diminishing. Then the scapegoated leader, feeling frustrated and alienated in the face of group resentment, believing that she had clarified her priorities for herself and they were not being supported by the group, left to begin new work.

Meetings became more directionless, awkward, and unfulfilling. Radicalesbians gradually abandoned all the forms the agenda so gloriously extolled. Each week, instead of fifty or sixty women, only fifteen or twenty would appear, many of these new women coming for the first time, never to be seen again. They probably wondered what the desultory, unfocused meeting was all about. It was impossible to recreate the group history for these women. There was always some business to attend to that had practical currency, and it seemed impossible to explain all the twists and turns of our group process. It had been a process to be lived, not one to be described or prescribed.

At this time, some members were very much locked into the need for weekly meetings because they perceived Radicalesbians as an organization whose membership came together once a week and could be counted on. There was also empathy for the women who were coming for the first time and trying to connect—lonely women, women with an urgent need for community and half-formed visions of a new lifestyle. It was felt that Radicalesbians had to provide a connecting point, a way of opening our embryonic community. Frantic efforts were made to keep the organization together despite the obvious absence of creative spontaneity. Trapped in an organizational mindset, unable to see any alternatives, some women became obsessed with revitalizing the weekly meetings that seemed to constitute the essence of Radicalesbians. Efforts were made to get the "dropouts" to return to meetings, and when that didn't work, anger, resentment and self-righteous denunciations were directed at these sisters for their apparent abandonment of the struggle.

During this time, the so-called dropouts, disheartened and devitalized by the alienating atmosphere of the large group rhetoric, had not just stopped attending meetings but had re-centered themselves in their consciousness-raising groups, where there were feelings of warmth and trust. These women also began to move out into other groups and activities that spoke to their political needs: squatters' actions, print-shop media centers, the Women's Center, the now women-controlled underground newspaper *RAT*, a newly formed Radicalesbian group in Philadelphia, and campus groups. Because of their negative experiences in the Radicalesbian weekly meetings, they carried the awareness that a dynamic of engagement and affinity was essential to their work.

When dialogue was re-established between "dropouts" and "hold-outs," what we came to realize was that old conceptions of organization had blinded us to the evolutionary process moving through us. A new gestalt had formed in the shape of our own needs and the connections we were making with each other that no organization could contain. Radicalesbians had been trying to fit a life force into an arbitrary form. There was a new realization that Radicalesbians was not a thing but a process, a flow, a way of looking at life from our own centers and trying to live in accordance with that self-knowledge. We saw the flow all around us in the changes we made in our lives: quitting our alienating, humiliating jobs; telling our parents and friends about our gay selves; moving into collectives to create chosen families; working on projects and activities that are alive and meaningful. Perhaps the voyage was launched from the weekly meetings, but the reality had become that women were leaving home and moving into new affinity and interest groups.

This is the "herstory" of the process that Radicalesbians underwent from 1970 to 1971 in New York City. During that time, spontaneously, lesbian-feminist groups formed all over the country, each undergoing its own evolutionary process. This explosion confirms that we were not an organization but a movement—a consciousness that continues to live and grow whenever it awakens in the hearts and minds of gay women.

L.A. Spring, 1970

KARLA JAY

IN the late Spring of 1970, much of the energy of the Los Angeles Gay Liberation Front (LA GLF) went into planning a march on June 28, the last Sunday of the month, to commemorate the one-year anniversary of the Stonewall Riots. Since a similar march was to take place in New York City, we decided to call ours the Christopher Street West Parade. We had raised enough money from the dances to cover our basic expenses, and a local group offered to put up $1,000 in bail money, enough to free about ten demonstrators, should they get arrested. No major event in Hollywood, of course, would be complete without floats. Several were proposed, one featuring two guys making out on a mattress (voted down), another with gay men and lesbians coming out of a closet—over and over, I presume, like an endless parade of clowns from a tiny car.

Our plans collapsed on June 10, when Police Chief Edward M. Davis refused to give us the necessary permits, demanding an impossible $15,000 from LA GLF for police overtime and insisting that we take out a policy for more than a million dollars in liability insurance and indemnity for protection against counter-protesters. He made things worse by telling the press that he would just as soon "discommode the people" by permitting a parade of "thieves and burglars." We didn't take kindly to the comparison.

At the last minute, the ACLU managed to overturn the restrictions, and we were permitted to march in the streets. We quickly pulled the event back together. Groups scrambled to create floats, which were more spontaneous and much bolder than we had originally planned. One sported a huge jar of Vaseline; another displayed a Christ-like figure tied to a cross with a sign that said: "In memory of those killed by the pigs." A hastily written flyer made the event sound like a hippie festival. We urged people to bring incense and musical instruments and to wear "Colorful Attire, Costumes, Flowers and Perfumes." Some people read the message as an invitation to a Halloween party or a drag ball. Men showed up in frilly dresses, clown suits, and fairy outfits that allowed the participants to seem both hip and outrageous while protecting them from being recognized by friends, colleagues, neighbors, and relatives. On the morning of the event, one fellow handed out pansies. At least one man wore an American flag (for which he could have been arrested). One gay man draped a seven-foot python around his muscular neck; an Amazonian lesbian rode a gigantic palomino.

We expected violence, and we felt that Chief Davis's linking us to common criminals might incite bystanders to attack us and even to feel justified about it. Most of us believed that, no matter how badly we were provoked, we should not respond in kind. Davis and his men were just looking for an excuse to beat or bust us. Others encouraged us to come armed. One cross-dresser told me he planned to carry a rifle under his skirt, making me think of the Mae West line, "Is that a gun in your pocket or are you just happy to see me?" (In this case, make that extremely happy.) I didn't think guns were the right solution, and I had never touched one.

ON the evening of the march, we lined up at six in the evening on the corner of Hawthorn and McCadden Place in the Hollywood area. It was eighty degrees and smoggy, as usual. I can't recall why we didn't march earlier in the day. Maybe no one wanted to forfeit a perfectly good beach day; it was a challenge to be political and to stay tan too. As we milled around waiting for the march to begin, we kissed and hugged one another. Here it was at last—our big moment! I knew we were making history, for never had such a large group of homosexuals taken to the streets. We passed out our GLF buttons, banners, and placards, printed with slogans addressing the evils of the Church, the State, and Ed Davis. A common theme (at a time when many of us referred derogatorily to heterosexuals as "breeders") was that homosexuality acted as a form of birth control. "More Deviation, Less Population," was a popular slogan before the lesbian baby boom.

At seven sharp, straight people's time, we began marching

East along Hollywood Boulevard toward Vine, singing songs about how if it was good enough for Sappho, it was good enough for us. (We were all essentialists then.) "Two, four, six, eight, how do you know your grandma's straight?" we chanted. We called out, "Give me a G, give me an A, give me a Y..." until we were hoarse from spelling out and shouting "Gay Power!" over and over. The MCC choir sang "Onward Christian Soldiers."

I started out in the front, carrying one pole of a GLF banner. I wasn't afraid of newsreels and photographs of the event reaching my family. I figured, correctly, that the march in New York would grab all the attention in the East. Still, I had an overwhelming sense of being watched and recorded. Police cameramen lined the sides and photographed everyone they could. Newspaper photographers sought out colorful clusters. There were over a thousand marchers—someone with a mechanical counter clocked exactly 1,169. Later, I learned that the New York march had included between three and five thousand participants, with some estimates even higher. I wished that I could have been at both events at once.

Spectators lined the sidewalks. At some places the crowd was ten deep. Most of the people cheered us on, and we responded by yelling, "Join us! Off of the sidewalks and into the streets!" Not all of the onlookers were friendly; some were there to jeer and curse us. One thing I had learned early on was to stay in the center of the crowd, as the people on the edges were most likely to get hit with flying debris. There were humorous moments as well. When a group from conservative Orange County carried a banner supporting Ronald Reagan, one woman in the crowd screamed that she didn't mind people being gay, but supporting Reagan was going too far!

The march seemed to go on for an eternity, although it couldn't have taken us more than an hour or two to traverse the mile-long route. We did have to stop regularly to allow cross-traffic through, and many of the native Angelinos were handicapped by never having walked a whole mile in their entire lives. After it was over, we were rather at a loss as to what to do. Because of the legal bickering, we had no time to plan a street party. The dance at Satan's we'd planned wouldn't start for another two hours.

Unlike the rest of us, Rev. Troy Perry was never at a loss for something to do. Like Morris Kight, he was a master at grabbing attention. Troy was still seething over Chief Davis' insulting remarks. Many whispered that Troy aspired to be our Martin Luther Queen. Davis presented him with an opening to launch the type of protest that that other martyred minister had made famous and vice-versa. What Troy didn't recognize was that part of King's strength was his originality. Troy was a poor imitation.

On June 14th, according to *The Advocate*, Troy, "with tears running down his cheeks," had told his congregation that he would begin a fast on the day of the march that would last until he had a pledge from public officials that they would work to get "these laws changed that discriminate against the homosexual in America." A man of his word, Troy traveled the parade route in a limousine, and then returned to the intersection of Hollywood Boulevard and Las Palmas, which was near the beginning of the march route, and sat down on a blanket on the sidewalk. (It was one thing to risk arrest, but getting his pants dirty was out of the question.) He was joined in his action by two women—Carol Shepherd, who was the president of the local Daughters of Bilitis (DOB) chapter, and Kelly Weiser, who represented a group called Homophile Effort for Legal Protection (HELP). By fasting, Troy was either making a grandiose gesture or planning on entering the *Guinness Book of Records* as the world's thinnest man.

At first, due to the dense crowds, no one spotted the three figures sitting on the curb as we danced by, even though Troy's black clerical garb stood out amid the sea of tie-dyed T-shirts. After the crowds had passed, all three were arrested for "malicious obstruction," a legal term that for me conjured images of clogged bowels.

Most of us didn't realize anyone had been arrested until Morris arrived at the GLF dance that evening at Satan's. In his officious manner, he ordered that the music be stopped so he could make an announcement. "Party pooper!" someone yelled out. Morris grabbed the mic and moved it to a central location. With his grandiloquent flair, Morris told us of Troy's arrest. I don't recall that he mentioned the women at all. The crowd quickly got worked up, and many of us, including Jim Kepner, Sandy Blixton, and I, starting making noises about driving to the Wilcox Avenue police station and staging a protest. After so many months of hard work, tedious planning, and legal wrangling, how could we do nothing about such a travesty of justice? Sandy, frustrated at failing to get a word in edgewise once again, shook his bottle of beer and sprayed it all over Morris. "Morris," Sandy announced, "You're all washed up."

Despite Sandy's dramatic interruption, the voices of moderation reigned. Several participants vowed to join Troy in his fast. A few people went to post bail for the three protesters. The two women accepted the quick release, but Troy refused and was kept in a cell overnight. According to his memoir, he spent the night alone, until he was joined by a drunk at 4 AM. His clerical collar probably protected him from being thrown into the tank.

Meanwhile, not to be outdone, a group of us went home, gathered our sleeping bags (every bona fide radical owned one) and some food, and returned to the same corner where the trio had been arrested. We were left undisturbed. Two men decided to stay the night, but after a while, the rest of us went home. The next day, after Troy was released on his own recognizance, he took his sit-in equipment—an air mattress, a blanket, water, and a Bible—to the steps of the Federal Building, which had already been the scene of other left-wing demonstrations. The change in venue was agreed upon as we would now be situated on land belonging to the Federal Government, where we believed we would be immune from arrest by Chief Davis' storm troopers. Some hoped that moving onto Federal property would propel our actions into the national limelight and that, after the sit-in, the media would regard Los Angeles, not New York, as the happening scene of gay liberation. In short, Troy and some of the others hoped the Federal Plaza would be our Selma.

THE Federal Plaza was in a downtown area nicknamed the "spaghetti bowl," because four or five huge interstate highways all crisscrossed there. One wrong lane, and you might find yourself in beautiful downtown Fresno. After a few hours, it looked like a tent city for homosexual hoboes. GLF members took three different positions regarding the sit-in. One faction, including Ralph S. Schaffer, the current GLF chair, joined the fast. A second faction, including me, joined the sit-in but not the fast. Fasting belonged to the realm of Buddhist meditative practices; the Federal Plaza seemed to me more suited for eating glazed donuts. A third group—the majority, in fact—felt that Troy was "grandstanding" or had simply taken a "no-win" stance. The action, they believed, could only end in arrest or surrender—in short, defeat.

The vigil on the steps of the Federal Building managed to be both riveting and dull at the same time. It was suspenseful because we had no idea what might happen at any moment, dull because nothing did happen. The Federal workers, for the most part, kept as far away from us as possible, avoiding our eyes, as if looking us in the face would be an admission of their own homosexuality. On some level, I felt as if I were in some encampment for the homeless, part of a community of societal pariahs that people would rather not see. Generally, we were left alone, and U.S. Marshall Gaylord L. Campbell—who had the most perfect name for the event: how many men can claim both "gay" and "camp" in their names?—told the press he had no intention of doing anything about our protest so long as it remained peaceful.

As a result, most of the time things were uneventful. Cameras appeared only when Troy called a press conference. He had already issued a press release about his arrest, complete with a handsome black-and-white photo of himself in clerical garb, standing against a brick wall. The press statement linked all the injustices that had been perpetrated on the local gay community: "Purposes of the fast are to esculate [*sic*] the removal of puritanica [*sic*] and repressive laws against sexual freedom; to protest the enticement and entrapment procedure of the police; to call attention to the tragic misunderstanding of homosexuals; and to ask that the community search its conscience in total reevaluation of its attitudes and ideas." The manifesto went on, somewhat illogically, to suggest that the action had some cataclysmic goal: "to save the world from total destruction." I did have to wonder whether Troy's seminary taught spelling; more seriously, I thought that pressing the issues beyond common reason wouldn't help our cause.

The sit-in dragged on. About once a day Troy called a press conference to refresh the memories of the fickle public, which was getting ready to flee to the beaches and hills for the Fourth of July weekend. Except for Troy, who went home to shower, usually more than once a day, the fasters were looking a lot grungier. They all looked thinner, especially Ralph, who was scrawny to begin with. About two days into the fast, some rumors began to fly around the Plaza that Troy was eating on the sly during his trips home. Angered, a few participants abandoned their fasts.

Most of the time, those who were fasting and those who were just hanging out and supporting the action, like myself, sat on the Plaza and tried to amuse ourselves. We didn't have any portable radios; this was before the era of Walkmen and boom boxes. We got to know each other really well by exchanging coming out stories, tales about where we had grown up, and anecdotes about our best and worst dates. One man read Tarot cards for everyone. I wasn't sure I wanted to know my immediate future, which probably involved bologna sandwiches on white bread and the manufacture of license plates. Occasionally, people came by with food, flowers, candles, or batteries for our flashlights.

I didn't do very well sleeping outdoors on the ground. My back was beginning to hurt a lot, and I longed for my own humble cooking. One evening Micki came by the Federal Plaza to visit, and I decided it was time to take a shower and have some sex, in that order. I was starting to feel—and smell—like an aged cheese. Back at Meredith's, I knew I couldn't return to the Federal Building to sleep. It was like breaking a spell or a fast; once I'd undone it, I couldn't imagine willfully torturing my body again.

On July 7, Troy publicly broke his fast, which had lasted ten days. By this time, he and other fasters looked terrible. Ralph looked as if he were about to disappear. Troy called a press conference and announced that he had gotten a "meaningful response from someone in authority interested in changing the laws that discriminate against homosexuals." Since Troy refused to name anyone and his statement was vague, I took this maneuver as his way of saving face. After all, it would take the entire legislature of almost every city and state to change the oppression his fast was intended to challenge. Moreover, Troy's actions were unpopular, even among many of his own parishioners. According to Jim Kepner, "Perry's fast on the Federal Building steps looked to conservative parishioners like a filthy hippie encampment." However, even though he had given up his fight in the face of waning public interest and the defection of some of the fasters—in the end only about seven were left—he did manage to hold out until people had come back from their holiday weekend.

Troy refused to admit defeat. He was determined to be acknowledged as our sacrificial lamb and earnest shepherd: In a carefully crafted scene worthy of Hollywood, he led a group of his supporters—mostly parishioners—back to the corner of Las Palmas and Hollywood Boulevard. Micki and I arrived just as Troy started passing around pieces of bread and then a cup of grape juice. Then everyone sang, "We Shall Overcome." If he had added even a touch of camp, I might have been able to get into it. I thought gay people should be a little more original.

I turned to Micki. "You know," I draped my arm around her shoulder. "Tell Anita that Scientology is looking better every day. Let's go to the beach, get fried, and then get wasted." And we did.

The first LA Pride Parade took place along Hollywood Boulevard on June 29, 1970. AP photo.

Fire Island: The Democratic Years

FELICE PICANO

WHAT was Fire Island Pines all about, and exactly who was included and who excluded? From 1965 to 1985, the years that I knew it, the Pines was one of eight or nine communities on a long sandbar that had grown at the edge of the Great South Bay, blocking the southern coast of central Long Island from the Atlantic Ocean.

Early communities on Fire Island go back to the turn of the 20th century. The Pines was settled much later, in the 1950s, as a "family community," but because of its picturesque little harbor and its central ridge almost sixty feet above the shoreline, it soon attracted those wanting to build houses with great outlooks and views. By the early '60s, the price of property and houses had risen above those of the other beach communities on the island. Architects and designers of note from New York, at the time the design center of the world, began to tear down beach cottages and erect "architectural statements" in their stead. Odd, grotesque, brilliant, experimental, some small but most large and a few monstrous—the houses had a kind of grand ephemerality about them, even the most solidly fortress-looking. Those on the beachfront were subject to hurricanes and tidal encroachments. No matter; soon people like Calvin Klein, Halston, and Angelo Donghia had places in the Pines, and they were followed by celebrities like Tommy Tune and James Levine. At the same time, the boats parked around and within the little harbor grew accordingly in size and luxury. Elizabeth Taylor, Nureyev, and Burt Reynolds could be seen being entertained upon their gargantuan decks.

The family community had become by 1968 a mixed community. The Sandpiper restaurant began to transform itself into a nightly dance club and attracted younger singles until 4 a.m. Unattached gay gentlemen with a lot of discretionary income bought or rented those former family houses, fixing them up to increasingly high standards. I first visited homes like this—a stock broker's rental—in the Pines when I was still a starving young writer. Already the place had begun to contrast sharply with the neighboring gay community, Cherry Grove, a more obviously working- and middle-class resort, where roughly equal numbers of men and women played. Nevertheless, despite the differences, interaction between the two communities was incessant.

By 1975, the era detailed in my memoir *A House on the Ocean, a House on the Bay*, many younger gay men and women had been "liberated" thanks to the impetus of the Stonewall riots, increased exposure about gay people in the media, and a heightened politicization. The newer generation, the "Stonewall babies," were by no means as affluent as their gay predecessors, but they were more numerous by far. Instead of alcohol, they tended to use recreational drugs like grass, LSD, coke, and early versions of Ecstasy. They listened and danced to rock, soul, and disco music rather than ballads and show tunes. Some, of course, were wealthy and had their own places, but most of the newcomers ganged up, sharing houses and even sharing rooms. As a result, suddenly there were a great many younger gay men, and to a lesser extent lesbians, visible in the Pines. Soon some members of the previous "Gin & Judy (Garland) Set" retreated to the Hamptons and other spots where liquor flowed freely.

This change represented a real democratization of gay life in the Pines. To be sure, celebrities still came out, and so did heirs to great fortunes like Johnson & Johnson and Campbell's Soup. But the run-of-the-mill Pines vacationer was more likely to be a thirty-year-old publishing editor, ad exec on the rise, or small business entrepreneur than a trust fund baby.

Rather than being racially elitist, the New York City gay scene that fed Fire Island Pines and Cherry Grove was one of the most Hispanic I've ever belonged to. Its main club off-season was Flamingo, named after Havana's famous nightclub of the '30s and '40s. Flamingo was the brainchild of Michael Fesco and a group of talented Caribbean, Central American, and South American gay men. During the era I write of, the Sandpiper—the main disco of the Pines—had as its head lighting person a Cuban, Jorge Maldonado, who worked alongside his lover, DJ Howard Merritt. Among the many guest DJ's at the Sandpiper were Junior, who came from the very ethnic Paradise Garage, and Flamingo's own Ritchie Rivera, who was also a talented record producer.

Twelve West and The Loft were the main feeders into Fire Island, which meant that their regulars would visit, stay in the Boatel, or find shares at Pines houses. With increased casual contact came more couples consisting of an Anglo and a Hispanic gay man. In my novel *Like People in History*, the narrator's two housemates are such a couple—as would have been natural in that era. Among my friends at the Pines were Puerto Ricans, Cubans, Dominicans, Colombians, Brazilians, and Venezuelans. Among the more colorful Pines characters were the artist Gustavo Novoa, the trannie runway model La Putassa, and the guy we called Santa Ana. Among the vast number of Pines-goers who died, probably a good third were men of Hispanic descent.

With African-Americans it was somewhat different, as might be expected in the America of that time—but not because of racist policies at Fire Island. To the contrary, I can recall being on the Manhattan-based Public Radio station with Isaac Jackson, an African-American, the night before the 1978 Gay Parade in New York City, the two of us exhorting black lesbians and gays—ostensibly numerous among his listeners—to join us the next day. Few did. Years later, writer Jewelle Gomez helped explain why, pointing out how deeply she and her African-American colleagues felt conflicted in those years between being black and being gay. Many of them had just settled into accepting "Black Pride"; going the step further to "Gay Pride" was seen as difficult, almost contradictory, given that many African-American leaders of the time characterized homosexuality as a "white disease."

Among my own African-American pals of that era—who were in the group Black and White Men Together and the BlackHeart Collective of writers—only Dave Frechette came out to Fire Island Pines occasionally. Because Dave was personable, smart, and funny (although by no means a "beauty"), he was, like the other gay black men out in the Pines, "laid, relaid, and parlaid," as he put it. Dave felt comfortable there and had fun. So did several other black gay men, like Bob Brasswell. When I tried to get Dave to invite out other pals of color, his comment was, "Sorry. Too much competition."

What's more, middle-class Hispanics and African-Americans were welcomed in the Pines. So were gays without much money at all—especially if they were attractive, sexy, friendly, or knew someone who had a place or a share on the island. Then there were those gay men, like my friend David "Miss Sherry" Jackson, who were willing to come out to the Pines on an early Saturday morning ferry and, in Sherry's words, "look for love or adventure." More than once I came upon him on the beach and invited him to sleep in our living room. "Don't bother," he'd say. "I like the challenge of finding a place on my own."

Because Fire Island was also a state and federal park, anyone with the price of a Long Island Railroad and ferry trip ticket could come for the day, use the beach, walk around, find love, lunch, dance, drink, dine, and return on the midnight boat. I never saw or heard of anyone refused entry. (It is true that there were no public toilets at the Pines Harbor unless you patronized those restaurants and bars, and this discouraged day-trippers with no money at all.)

Far from excluding eighty percent of potential visitors, then, the Pines excluded virtually no one at all. Of course, there's a difference between just being there on whatever terms and being part of the in-crowd, the "A list." And yet, to draw from my own experience, it wasn't until almost two decades later, at a dinner party in California, at which I was reintroduced to an old Pines acquaintance, that I heard him say, "Felice was part of the A-crowd, but he was always nice to me." I was never aware of any such classism, much less that I was considered to be on the A list. I simply hung out in the Pines with my usual city friends, although I sought romance and sex among the entire population, the way most gay men did and still do. I'm reminded of another friend who strove so hard to join the private club Flamingo in 1979. "But you can't dance," I argued with my pal, "You dress badly. You don't do drugs. And you're terrible sex! Why would you want to join a club that emphasizes all of your shortcomings?" His answer was simple: because everyone else wanted to join.

And let's not forget that there were various elderly, physically out-of-shape, and by no means model-attractive guys who frequented the Pines year after year. One such retirement-age personality wore a transparently obvious wig and multiple gold chains around his wrinkled neck, and sported distinct cardiac bypass scars on his eternally bared, tanned-out-of-a-bottle chest. Whenever he entered Tea Dance people would welcome him with the chant, "Here comes Spare Parts!" Mean, you say? Perhaps. But it was also accurate and affectionate. Spare Parts would always smile, wave regally, then proceed to dance and otherwise enjoy his local fame.

Jill Johnston in Los Angeles, ca. 1978. Suzan Cooke photo.

Was Lesbian Separatism Inevitable?

JILL JOHNSTON

LESBIAN Nation *is one of those books whose title said it all. The book itself is a series of essays published in* The Village Voice *from 1969 to 1972, written in the brash, brilliant, free-associating style for which Johnston is famous—but it quickly became a "manifesto" for a segment of the population that was only beginning to come out in large numbers and get organized in 1973, just four years after the Stonewall Riots. The title became a rallying cry and a symbol of solidarity for those in the vanguard of this new movement, and their followers.*

The book's subtitle, "The Feminist Solution," referred to a dilemma of identity and political organizing that vexed many lesbians at the time: whether to honor their status as women by working with the burgeoning feminist movement, or whether to honor their lesbianism by joining the growing but increasingly male-dominated gay rights movement. Johnston's solution was one that embodied both a stinging indictment of "the patriarchy" in all its manifestations and a stern critique of the straight feminist movement, which had witnessed periodic outbursts of anti-lesbian sentiment. The concept of a "lesbian nation" proposed a separation from both movements in favor of a radical brand of feminism in which men played almost no role—a feminism for women who needed only the company of other women And not only out lesbians were invited to this party: "All women are lesbians except those who don't know it," Johnston famously wrote.

As a manifesto, Lesbian Nation *has been credited with launching the lesbian separatism that produced, as the 70s wore on, a bumper crop of lesbian communes, coffeehouses, bookstores, and music festivals in the U.S. and Canada. Whether that was its intent is not entirely clear. With chapter titles like "The Second Sucks and the Feminine Mystake" and "Amazons and Archedykes," the book was as much about wordplay and satire as it was about launching a separatist subculture. Indeed the often experimental writing was pitched at a high level of difficulty and complexity, hardly the stuff of political pamphleteering.*

For all the historical importance of Lesbian Nation, *the period of writing that produced it was in some ways a long detour for Johnston, who started life as a dance critic and resumed her career as an art critic in the 1990s, turning especially to the visual arts with books such as* Jasper Johns *and* Secret Lives in Art. *In the interim, she produced a two-part autobiography (*Mother Bound *and* Paper Daughter*). A collection published in 1988,* Admission Accomplished: The Lesbian Nation Years *(1970–75), compiles Johnston's essays during this five-year period and demonstrates in 56 essays the breadth of her interests, which ranged from misogyny and same-sex marriage to language and literature.*

This interview was conducted by the G&LR *editor via e-mail in January 2006.*

The Gay & Lesbian Review: This issue of the *G&LR* is focusing on some of the major turning points in the early rise of gay and lesbian culture. Your book, *Lesbian Nation,* was a landmark during this period (the early 1970s) and became a manifesto for lesbian politics and organization. The book emerged out of a series of essays you wrote for *The Village Voice*. How did this series come about, and what role did the *Voice* play in these turbulent times?

Jill Johnston: *Lesbian Nation,* it's true, emerged out of writings in *The Village Voice*—that would have been between 1969 and 1972. But these writings, which were technically columns, could only be said to have emerged from a prior ten-year involvement at the paper.

I began at the paper as a critic, in 1959, writing reviews and opinions about dance, art, happenings, Intermedia, the avant-garde generally, when the paper was just four years old. In the mid-'60s, an upheaval in my life turned me away from criticism to a running account of my adventures from week to week. These were daringly published by the *Voice,* even as my writing became more and more a-grammatical, disregarding all the textbook conventions. By 1968, this curious form was established, and was quite popular in the art world. In 1969, a few women in the GLF [Gay

Liberation Front], finding me writing about my travels cross-country with a young woman, correctly divining that she was a lover, invited me to their meetings at a church on Ninth Avenue in Manhattan. And what followed became, as they say, history. Having been schooled in all the art forms, being very apolitical, I had a lot of resistance at first, especially to understanding the status of women in political terms. I had not a clue, in fact, that the genders were so seriously segregated, to the historical disadvantage of women. The fact that certain women, called lesbians, were outcasts, was not hard to get. So I started there.

The role, I would say, that the *Voice* played in "those turbulent times" as regarded my part in them was that it continued to publish me. It seems I became good copy. During the early '70s they received hundreds of letters to the editor about my column. I received hundreds of them myself. And I never wrote about sex per se, by the way. It was just the L-word that did it. I can't discount, however, the appeal of the craziness of my adventures—for example, encounters on the road on book tours with hostile crowds and raucous claques.

G&LR: Maybe you could talk a little about the historical and cultural backdrop out of which you developed your ideas about feminism and lesbian separatism. The anti-war movement and the counterculture were in full swing: what impact did they have?

JJ: Once I understood the feminist doctrines, a lesbian separatist position seemed the commonsensical position, especially since, conveniently, I was an L-person. Women wanted to remove their support from men, the "enemy," in a movement for reform, power, and self-determination. A revolutionary prototype existed in their midst. But the prejudice against women within the ranks of women, much less loving women at the intimate level, was so great (and still is, of course) that feminists could only act against their own best interests and trash the women who modeled their beliefs. The split between straight feminists and lesbian feminists was extremely damaging, and will no doubt continue to be in any future wave, to the cause of women's liberation. The internal damage within the lesbian feminist ranks was also lethal.

You ask about the backdrop of the antiwar movement and counterculture. The huge turmoil in the 1960s produced an atmosphere of insurrection generally. That's where we all came in. The media were making money off it, and book contracts were being handed out. The feminist movement was male-supported, defined, and perpetuated right down to the barricades. *Lesbian Nation* was bought by a male editor, titled by him, and produced and publicized by his male-owned corporation (Simon & Schuster). We were all agreeable, sometimes enthusiastic, employees. Money and exploitation aside, the men were information-gathering, finding out what we thought, what we were up to, how far we could go, and what concessions might be made by society and government before we were shut down.

G&LR: To what extent was the concept of a "lesbian nation" a literal concept, i.e. a vision of a world of women living lives independent of men? The ideas developed in the book helped to inspire the communitarian movement and separatist organizing of the 1970s. Can you talk a little about some of these experiments and organizing efforts?
JJ: In a revolutionary time, separatism is inevitable. An oppressed group of people first must gather together to define themselves and seek mutual support. A "vision of a world of women living independently of men" was not a realistic, indeterminately future one. It was rather a stage in the process. Black separatism had the same profile. I see a number of stages like this (provided the earth survives) until the oppressor group ceases to exist as such. Straight women in the '70s, of course, left their husbands and boyfriends in droves, many of them coming out, or trying to. Separatism was hardly carried out just by lesbians, all perceptions to the contrary. Merging was going on, and lines blurred. But at heart the women's liberation movement was one of reform, not revolution. Clamoring to get a better deal under patriarchy isn't a bad way to define it.

G&LR: *Lesbian Nation* came at a time when both the women's movement and the gay and lesbian rights movement were in their infancy. Lesbians had divided loyalties because of their dual minority status. The book seemed to counsel women to move away from the world of men, including the male-dominated gay rights movement. Is this an accurate reading?
JJ: Yes, the women in the lesbian/feminist movement were defining themselves independently of men, including gay men. However, *Lesbian Nation* had the imprimatur of the mainstream mass

media, which helped create consensus and identity. For example, copies of the book took up the entire window display of Brentano's on Fifth Avenue.

G&LR: When the book was published, it quickly became a cultural event. How would you describe the reaction to the book in general? Why do you think the book had this kind of impact?
JJ: I can't really answer your questions about the impact and results of *Lesbian Nation*. I was too much in the middle of it, and trying to survive its publication. As a writer, as which I chiefly identify myself, survival has been difficult to say the least.

G&LR: You obviously continued writing long after *Lesbian Nation* was published. How did your own thinking about feminism and GLBT rights issues evolve in the ensuing years? To what extent have you modified the central views you expressed in the book?
JJ: I haven't modified anything I said in the book. I just don't say it any more. As an evolving writer, however, the *way* it was written now looks weird to me. I've been through a number of stages of writing, subject and style-wise, since then. Those several years naturally influenced my future writing, though it's often hard to see how exactly, when the attitudes appear transformed in new subjects.

G&LR: How would you characterize the significance of the book in the larger context of the 1970s and the GLBT rights movement? What would you say was the long-term impact of the book from a vantage point of thirty-plus years?
JJ: I have no idea about any significance of *Lesbian Nation* in context of the GLBT rights movement. I personally am firmly lined up behind civil rights for gay men and lesbians. At the same time, I have otherwise always found the link between us weak to non-existent. Gay men, however discriminated against, are still patriarchs. My alignment was always with the women, across all lines. Personally, again and however, I had a number of male friends back then, and still do. I have a son Richard and a grandson Ben, among other male relatives and friends.

As the '70s World Turned

ANDREW HOLLERAN

EDITOR'S NOTE: This is the second part of Andrew Holleran's essay, "My Harvard," which ran in the very first issue of The Harvard Gay & Lesbian Review *(Winter 1994). In Part 1, Holleran discussed his years as an undergraduate at Harvard in the 1960s, focusing especially on two classmates: Richard (Dick), a shy, eccentric English major; and Joel, a confident, ambitious artist from New York. He also discussed two books that had made an impression: Erik Erikson's* Childhood and Society *(1963), which argues that there are certain crises in life that we all must meet, one of which is "the Crisis of Intimacy"; and Henry James' novel* The Ambassadors, *in particular a scene in which an older man whom life has passed by tells a younger man: "Live all you can—it's a mistake not to."*

YEARS later, the dear friends I couldn't bear to part with in June of 1965 were all leading separate lives. The math major from Oregon got married, took over the family farm, and had two daughters. The friend who wanted to visit Cape Sounion with his bride did so. Joel moved to Paris, met someone, he wrote in a letter, "who sees the world the way I do," and began trying to earn a living. Richard moved to Washington, D.C., to avoid the draft, and taught high school. I took the foreign service exam, thinking I would work for the State Department; but each time I scheduled a personal interview, I canceled—thinking the FBI or whoever interviewed me would know I wasn't straight. (As Gore Vidal said: "I could've been President except for the fag thing!") Instead, I went to a writer's workshop—who cared, in the arts, if you were gay?—and after a stint in the Army, moved to New York and became a clone. The few times Joel and I got together on one of his trips back home, our relationship seemed a bit awkward; it was obvious we couldn't reproduce Harvard on the streets of Greenwich Village.

He hated New York, for one thing. I loved it. He wasn't "gay." I was. The period of hilarious innocence was over, and Harvard was behind us, and everything had to be, in a sense, renegotiated.

One summer evening, we were walking through Greenwich Village while he was in New York on business eating ice cream cones, the way we had in Cambridge, and we passed a newsstand. Writers in the newsmagazines at that time—1975—were fond of saying the love that dared not speak its name now would not shut up. In the ten years since Joel and I had graduated, not only had I come out of the closet, so had thousands of other people. I even knew the man with whom Joel had gone to Europe the summer after I'd met Joel and Dick—a French teacher who now lived three blocks from me in the East Village, where, though he never visited the bars and discos I did, he lived with one lover after another, always Puerto Rican or black, like some man in a story by Joseph Conrad, one Conrad never wrote. Joel of course had been with the same companion for ten years now; without ever once having gone to a bar, bath, or place like Fire Island—the three staples of my existence at that time, places one went ostensibly to find a companion, again and again and again. Which was the reason I felt a little embarrassed taking him down Christopher Street that evening: Part of me was wondering if he hadn't done it in a better way, and didn't consider this pathetic.

In fact, by 1975, Christopher Street had turned fairly trashy, the excesses of the '70s already beginning to transform it into something seedy; and as we walked it all seemed suddenly sordid in a way that it might not have had I not been trying to sense, as we walked, his reaction. I was already anticipating his disapproval, perhaps, the failure of the scene to match his own standards in life, whether this was Harvard snobbery or Harvard intelligence, when we passed a newspaper stand covered with porn magazines like *Honcho*, *Mandate*, and *Drummer*. Joel stopped for a moment to look at them, and then said, as we walked on, in a musing voice: "Why do they make so much of it over here?"

Why *do* we make so much of it over here, indeed? The question struck me then, and still does: I'd made a lot of it, certainly, in my own life. It had become in a sense everything. So I had to ask my own self what he had, what only a visitor, perhaps, could. The easy answer to his question was to say that in Europe, homosexuality was not the basis for a separate category, community, self-interest group that it was here; that people there lived out their sexual preference while remaining in the context of the larger society and culture. And that you could call this either staying in the closet, or refusing to be ghettoized. What was this mob scene I was involved in, anyway, this stampede of promiscuity, this gay life that seemed all too often toward the end of the '70s as predictable and conformist as any in the suburbs, with its rituals, habits, stereotypes, expectations, and burn-out? Perhaps homosexuality was in fact an essentially private and personal fact, something that had to do with the person in one's bed, and nothing more. I could have told Joel that it was a French man, Renaud Camus, who'd written a book that described gay life as well as any I'd read, a book aptly named *Tricks*. But that was not the answer. So I was back to his simple question as we strolled onto the pier: Why did we make so much of it over here?

NOTHING is so diminishing as to realize that one was, after all, part of a trend—an era, a historical moment. American life—the sort journalists sum up in decades, or nicknames—is something that Harvard people think, I suspect, they are too smart for, too individual, too different, to be a part of. But I was part of something, I guess, that Joel was not. The Age of Clones, 1971 to 1979 AD. All movements are merely accumulations of many individuals desiring the same thing, of course. When you are coming out, you do not spend much time thinking about what you are doing—you want simply to live, to have a personal life—an approximation at first of the dreams one was brought up with: domestic happiness, fidelity, affection, trust. You want to solve what Erik Erikson called "the Crisis of Intimacy."

These concepts translate oddly into homosexual life, I learned. There was no education for the sort of life I ended up leading. We are not brought up to be gay. There was a sense of learning new codes, living in New York as a gay man; of going to school all over again in a society that did not recognize the diploma you'd earned. It recognized other things, mostly unrelated to your education—exactly the problem of all education, Henry Adams had pointed out. I, who wondered what Henry James had meant in *The Ambassadors*, was now wondering how to combine brewers' yeast with my morning milkshake because I needed extra protein for the body-building I was doing at the gym. The thing that had not seemed important at Harvard—the body—was now crucial. My roommate would not travel unless he could continue his workouts wherever he was going, as if he were afraid he would deflate.

Life in the '70s was an extraordinary burst of energy and invention. But questions of history and literature were replaced by three: Did you go out last night? Who was there? How was the music? (I did. It was jammed. The music was okay.) In 1977, a Harvard graduate named Toby Marotta came out in his 10th Anniversary Class Report. He got so many letters, he wrote a book called *Sons of Harvard*—a collection of interviews with gay classmates. One weekend I went down to Washington to visit Richard—Richard who, with classic New England reserve, had never said a word about his private life. Neither Joel nor I had any idea about his sexuality or amorous life. All we knew was that he had been in therapy and was living with nineteen cats. One summer evening he and I stood on a terrace of the Capitol, and I asked him what he wanted out of life, and he said: "I want to be successful and have a family." The words stunned me, and not only because he seemed far from this goal. When I said goodbye as he dropped me off at Union Station, I did not tell him I felt like the Little Mermaid returning to the sea—the sea of men. I was addicted to cruising. Ten years after graduation from Harvard, where I saw nothing in terms of sex, I now saw everything that way. Re-reading *The Ambassadors*, it struck me that the book was really about Chad Newsome's penis—everyone wanted it. And instead of going to Paris to live, live all I could, I headed straight for the Everard Baths the moment the train returned me to New York.

One night, the Everard burned down. People died, it was said, because the owners had not hooked up the sprinklers. One of the dead was the lover of a man from my neighborhood that I used to run into every now and then, infrequently, because he spent six months of the year teaching English in Saudi Arabia and six months back in New York, since, he said, he needed half a year in a strict, puritanical, drugless society to alternate with New York. It was true that, having no limits thanks to penicillin, there seemed no way the escalation of drugs, muscles, ways to have sex, would stop. The Everard was rebuilt, and now there was also the St. Marks, Man's Country, and The Club. I was reading Henry James now in the waiting room of the Enteric Disease Clinic on 9th Avenue, where I kept running into friends, while waiting for our shit to be analyzed for amoebas. Once I overheard the nurse ask one of the patients the usual question, "Have you been traveling?" and I thought: Yes, in all the wrong circles.

Yet the moment one was cured, one celebrated by going back into the fray. As a friend said when I asked him what he was going to do with his clean bill of health: "Go to the Mineshaft." In the meantime, a new generation arrived in the City that wanted nothing to do with discos, plaid shirts, or Fire Island theme parties. One day I looked down and saw stenciled on the sidewalk of my block by a group called Fags Against Facial Hair the words "CLONES GO HOME." I obeyed. Burned out by it all, I went home and ended up writing a book about an experience that seemed to have nothing to do with what I'd been educated or prepared for: gay life. An experience that constituted an odd, mostly invisible, and very foreign country all by itself.

Oddly, all three of us had ended up living apart—Dick in the inner city of Washington, Joel in Paris, me in gay America, all equally foreign somehow. What was wonderful was our friendships surviving everything. The awkward reunions spaced over a decade eventually worked themselves out. Joel even introduced me to a man in New York—a friend of his—who became my closest friend in New York. They were pleased about my getting published. We walked around New York together, the three of us, soon after this. Then AIDS hit in 1983, and took the friend Joel had introduced me to, and the next thing I heard were long-distance calls from Paris and Washington asking how I was.

San Francisco: Still Mighty Real

JEWELLE GOMEZ

A GIRLFRIEND and I were walking amiably on Castro Street in the fall afternoon sun, or at least in the patches we could find as we weaved in and out of the groups of gay men that bustled and hustled on the sidewalk. It was 1988, I was visiting from New York and my old friend was trying to convince me to move west. Not much of a struggle—I'd been in love with San Francisco since I was ten years old and my great-grandmother first showed me a packet of postcards she'd saved from a trip West a decade before. It was a set of those pastel-tinted cards with breathtaking views, that make me think of cream-filled candies, convertible roadsters, and happy endings. For years I used to rummage through my great-grandmother's bureau drawer to pull the cards out and revisit that place I'd never been.

The corner of Castro and 18th Street was probably one of the most congested intersections in the Western Hemisphere during the 1980s. It reminded me of those postcards in many ways. With its grease-stained sidewalks and disco undercurrent, the Castro's resemblance to romantic postcards is not immediately obvious. There is something familiar, however, in how the dreams of generations of people, gay and straight, have been painted into that tiny space. Some of the dreams will come true, others will be just souvenirs of a long ago trip.

On that fall day we were crossing 18th Street when we neared a youngish white man, probably about 25 years old. He said, as we approached, "Can you spare some change? So I can get back home to Ohio?" Both of us said in unison and without hesitation,

"Why?" In retrospect, it was a callous response. But the core of our question was not a dismissal of the man's plight nor of the Buckeye state. It was a gut response from our own deeply-held sense of being at home in this Oz of a city, in that slightly seedy postcard of a neighborhood. At that moment neither of us could imagine going back to where ever it was we'd escaped from to get to the Castro.

But I did go back to New York City, and it was four more years before I actually migrated to the West Coast. I came over on the Mayflower. Or at least all my boxes, books, and clothes did, on a Mayflower truck that arrived a week after me. Traumatized by the passage away from forty years as an Easterner, I spent my first month in San Francisco inside the house, unpacking and washing my great-grandmother's glassware and shelving my books. It helped ease my disorientation at finding myself at the other end of the continent with Mediterranean-like sunlight, even in the winter. I needed some time to accept that sitting by the ocean meant watching the sunset and not the sunrise.

One way my partner, Diane, helped me to reorient myself was to take me for drives around the city in the evening and always we'd finish our perambulations by driving through the Castro on our way home. And each time we'd drive up Castro Street the neighborhood would become more and more familiar to me. I'd recognize the shops, the people, and the landscape as the one I've often imagined.

The only landmark I knew with any certainty was the bookstore, A Different Light. It was the one place I'd always come when I visited. I'd go inside, pretending I was looking at the books—my own or others'. But what I mostly did was just feel the people around me. I took them the different pacing and energy, other's sense of the city, the neighborhood, grounded myself in what it felt like to be in the Castro and actually be a part of the postcard. Maybe not the one my great-grandmother had cherished, but my own version.

The Castro, as I came to know it, was quite different from what I'd imagined. From my perspective on the East Coast through the 1970s and '80s, the Castro had one face. It was white, neatly bearded, and condescending. The several times I had visited before 1988, I would walk around the city and inevitably when I got to the Castro it was only in the bookstore that I felt at home. On the street I was invisible. I was black and a woman, the least valuable commodity in the Castro.

It was a distinctly frustrating experience to feel eyes slide past me as if I wasn't there. Whatever activist impulses and sense of community I had developed through working with various GLBT groups over the previous years were not mirrored in the crowds on Castro Street. Affordable housing, human rights, world peace, comparable worth all seemed like quaint issues, relegated to discussion by only the un-buff throwbacks over in Berkeley. Castro Street palpitated with the rhythm of cruising, and male desire had a very specific beat, leaving no room for anything else. Sisterhood may have been powerful but no one in the Castro was interested in finding out about it.

I minded being invisible in the city that Harvey Milk's martyrdom had made seem like the center of social change. I wanted to see the political boys who'd turned the night white with their anger. What I saw in those early visits, however, was averted faces, all coyness and calculation. When I saw Marlon Riggs' film *Tongues Untied*, I understood his anger as a black man at that invisibility. I didn't care about not being an object of desire, in fact it was one of the benefits of walking around the Castro. It was a relief not to feel like a piece of flesh on display for men all the time. But for Riggs and other black men, it was spit in their faces. The sweating, pulsing, energy of sexual freedom was on in the air but not really available to them. They were still a dark secret, kept in its place.

On those first visits I was disappointed that the political outrage I'd seen in the *Harvey Milk* documentary and heard about in Stonewall stories didn't seem to translate into a daily political consciousness or a sense of a progressive community when I walked in the Castro (not that they did in Greenwich Village either). But I could always hang out at A Different Light bookstore, where the books and those who loved them created an aura of unity, at least in that particular little space.

During my visit in 1988, though, things had begun to change. Death had taken its toll. The virus had swept up Castro Street with its scythe and the crowds of handsome young men had been thinned. With the plague came a call to arms that was answered by all types of queer people; and a sense of real political unity seemed to be forged for the first time. When I walked in the Castro I no longer had to step out of the way of men who didn't see me.

Later that weekend, I attended a rally celebrating disco star Sylvester, who lay ill in his apartment near Castro Street. I walked from the Mission across 18th Street to the Castro and on the way saw, spray-painted on the sidewalk, the words "KILL NIGGERS." My first reaction was that someone had slipped in from out-of-town to deface the city. I was still seeing San Francisco from the perspective of those pastel postcards. I caught my breath and looked around, wondering if someone else would come along and witness this obscenity. For once 18th Street by Dolores Street was quiet, and I was alone with my outrage and fear. My heart beat fast as if who ever had scrawled their hatred on the sidewalk might be hidden behind a lace curtain, taking aim at me. I was first hurt, then angry. But there was no one around so the anger retreated inside somewhere, that unsettled place where rage lives.

Rage is always hidden beneath the surface for most people of color, even here in the postcard. When I walk west toward the Castro what comes to my mind is not just the lovely Spanish-style mission visited by thousands of tourists on Dolores Street. Nor do I first think of the new inhabitants—some with SUVs, others with black nail polish and multiple piercings—who think they invented the Mission and the Castro. I think of missionaries. Their complicity in the decimation of Indians that populated the land rises up over me like a chilly shadow when the sun ducks behind the clouds. They are not so easily gotten rid of as the missionaries thought. I feel the Ohlone people around me watching. When I read the hateful graffiti on the street I cringe for myself and for the people the land has not forgotten.

A critic who reviewed a book of mine once observed that often the characters in my work are escaping to the West. I hadn't noticed that until I read the article. The reviewer, not knowing me and following an impersonal political instinct, mistakenly attributed my facing West to some sublimated expansionist leanings that I hadn't examined fully. I tend to think that because my own family tree holds the Ioway as well as Wampanoag tribe, my yearning to come West are connected to a deeper impulse.

Somewhere inside I feel I'm returning to a land (metaphorically speaking) I've known or that's known me. This makes the insidious hatred of the anonymous author of the sidewalk scrawl all the more wounding. It's hatred for the me—"black, brown, red, or yellow"—who belongs to this land.

When I finally get to the Sylvester celebration at the intersection of Castro and Market Streets I leave the anger and disappointment behind. The people who mill around are an interesting mix of what I would expect—people of all colors *and* all colors of hair. Outfits are eclectic—leather, gingham, denim and many are just the thing to make Sylvester proud, all that was needed was a glitter ball over head. Like many of the other people there tears well up and run down my cheeks. I feel immensely sad to be about to lose such a talent and generous spirit in our community. I also feel stricken that the one Black Queen who's been able to reign in the Castro will no longer hold sway. I immerse myself in the crowd that chants "We love you Sylvester," hoping it's loud enough for him to hear in his sickbed. Our voices bind together to make one sound and we can't stop chanting, as if the words are a lifeline that will keep him with us.

Part IV

Stonewall's Legacy: Whither the Revolution?

Stonewall's Legacy

RICHARD SCHNEIDER JR.

THE *Gay & Lesbian Review* came into being amid an epic debate that was in full swing in the early 1990s over the state and direction of the LGBT movement. With the 25th anniversary of Stonewall in the background, it was perhaps a generational shift that writers were noticing and that was in fact taking place, one that Michael Bronski summed up (in *The G&LR*'s Winter 1994 issue) as a shift from "sexual liberation" to "identity politics" as the guiding model of political action. The former was the vision that had held sway from the post-Stonewall era through ACT UP and into the '90s; the latter was being embraced by well-funded organizations like the Gay & Lesbian Task Force and the Human Rights Campaign, which expressly rejected the earlier revolutionary goals. This debate was remarkable both for its passion and for its volume (as in volumes published), and also the extent to which it became polarized between these two positions.

It didn't take long for *The G&LR* to get into the act. Our second issue featured an "open letter" from David Bergman (our longtime poetry editor) critiquing a book by Bruce Bawer titled *A Place at the Table* (1993), which argued that the gay movement should stop trying to change the world and instead focus on achieving basic civil rights as other minorities have. Bergman objected that this would be a formula for allowing dutiful, law-abiding citizens to sit at the table while relegating everyone else to the margins. And who said we *want* to be at their table, anyway?

That question, or a version of it, was at the heart of the argument. Identity politics was all about being allowed to participate fully in institutions such as marriage and military service that were closed to LGBT people. Someone like conservative pundit Andrew Sullivan became an early advocate of marriage equality; his argument was that the goal should stop at full legal equality, while sexual orientation ought to be irrelevant to a person's public life. In contrast, the writers in this section—all activists who can remember the days of "gay liberation"—tend to regard the marriage quest as emblematic of the abrogation of the "spirit of Stonewall" in favor of an assimilationist agenda.

As Bronski points out in his 1995 piece, the "identity" model simply adopted the tried-and-true politics of African-Americans and women by redefining LGBT people as a minority group in need of legal protection. He associates the sexual liberation model with *behavior* as distinct from identity; it was sexual practice that needed to be liberated from the straightjacket of puritanism—for everyone. In contrast, the identity model, in order to make the case that sexual orientation is involuntary and immutable, had to adopt a highly essentialist position captured by the title of Lady Gaga's song "Born This Way." Altering the metaphor, Frank Browning characterized this shift as a transition from the language of "desire" to the language of "pride" (Spring 1998).

Other pieces that appeared in *The G&LR* in the '90s characterized this shift in various ways. Arnie Kantrowitz focused on the growing commercialization of gay culture; and indeed it was in the '90s that there suddenly arose a host of slickly produced magazines (*OUT*, *Genre*, *Curve*, et al.), gay travel companies and cruise lines, LGBT movies and film festivals, and the "gay publishing boom." In a similar vein, Dennis Altman recalls that the old liberation ethos included a critique of capitalism and inequality along with a rejection of repressive sex codes and anti-gay discrimination.

The articles in this section form two clusters (not that it was planned this way): the writers mentioned above from our early years (1994–99) and a group from more recent issues, with a gap of almost fifteen years in between. Those in the first group were in the trenches, acutely aware that a change of course was underway, and on balance they were not sanguine about this trend. The recent writers are looking back on changes that were inchoate in the '90s but now look like a fait accompli. LGBT people can now serve in the military, get married, adopt children, move out to the suburbs, and so on. The collective sigh that one hears from these writers is a nod to the importance of these accomplishments mixed with a sense that something has been lost in the bargain.

Perhaps the clearest expression of this critique is that of D. Gilson, who coins the term "homonormativity" to describe an idealized LGBT community that has indeed achieved equality with the hetero majority, but which is disproportionately white, male, and affluent, excluding many slices of the queer community. Dolores Klaich expands on this theme by showing how each gain in LGBT equality comes at a cost. Thus, for example, marriage equality is a great achievement, and marriage really does confer advantages—which means that unmarried gay people will be further marginalized vis-à-vis the larger community.

Amy Hoffman in a piece titled "The Quest for Identity" raises the basic question of what it means to base one's identity on a sexual orientation. What if one is closeted in some contexts but out in others? What if the social constructionists are right and "gay" and "straight" are just socially defined categories; are we then just succumbing to society's controls? As if to answer this, Larry Kramer launches a screed against the entire edifice of Queer Theory and social constructionism, which insists that gay identity is a recent invention that cannot be mapped onto other cultures.

Kramer, of course, is an unreconstructed essentialist, as are most people outside of academia, where the theories of Michel Foucault (Eve Sedgwick, Judith Butler, et al.) still predominate. Which is somewhat remarkable, given that an unspoken essentialism has been the dominant ideology of the mainstream LGBT movement for decades. The underlying assumption of the identity model is that sexual orientation is a fixed trait analogous to race or gender, and this doctrine has proven highly effective as a strategy for securing such rights as military service and marriage equality.

But lest we get too comfortable, recent developments point to another shift in consciousness as a new generation comes of age. The main struggle today is for transgender rights, and indeed the whole concept of gender as a binary system has come under close scrutiny. Sexual orientation, too, is seen as a more slippery concept than advertised, with Millennials resistant to labels of all kinds, and the concept of "sexual fluidity" back in fashion. Indeed the new mindset can seem remarkably reminiscent of the zeitgeist of the early gay liberation era, when a favorite slogan was "Hey, hey, what d'ya say? Try it once the other way!" The notion that gender and sexuality are fluid and variable and subject to whim is not a new idea. The wheel keeps turning.

Protesters outside the U.S. Supreme Court in April 2015 in the run-up to the decision in June that legalized same-sex marriage. A giant banner combined American symbolism with the rainbow flag of Gay Pride. Paul J. Richards/AFP/Getty Images.

Sexual Liberation Versus Identity Politics

MICHAEL BRONSKI

THE Stonewall Riots were the beginning and in many ways the defining moment of the contemporary gay and lesbian liberation movement. Although such homophile groups as Mattachine and the Daughters of Bilitis existed in the 1950s and '60s, it was at Stonewall that actual revolt took place, and the anger, dammed up for so long, broke free and spilled out onto the streets.

It is important, before talking about the future, to remember something about the past. The Stonewall Riots and the Gay Liberation Front would not have happened in 1969 had it not been for the enormous social vitality of the times. If it were not for the presence of the Black Power movement, the Second Wave of feminism, the youth culture, the Civil Rights movement, the drug culture, hippies, and rock and roll, the raid on the Stonewall Inn would have been one more petty police harassment against one more mob-owned drinking hole. It's important not to forget that the phrase "gay liberation" that came so quickly to our lips was a tribute to the existing cultural power of "women's liberation." Nor should we forget that the actions that erupted on Christopher Street that night were fueled by the energy of rock and roll and the drug culture, as well as the entire street culture that existed in Greenwich Village in the 1960s, which was quite different from the urban decay and homelessness that exist today [in 1994]. Draconian city and state economic policies had yet to turn street culture into the nightmare it is today.

All of these social movements and cultural manifestations were born of a desire to be able to behave in ways that were proscribed by social norms—"Do your own thing," in the parlance of the time. The Civil Rights movement demanded that people of color have the right of access allowed white people and not be penalized for it: the right to sit anywhere on the bus; the right to walk down the street and not be greeted by fear and suspicion. The women's movement demanded that women have the right to control their own bodies in matters of sex, not to be forced to have children they didn't want, and to behave as they liked in public without fear of harassment by men. The youth and drug cultures were predicated on seeking the right to experiment with and enjoy our bodies however we saw fit. In line with all this, the impulse behind the gay liberation movement was to have the freedom to *behave* homosexually—to have sex without worry of arrest or harassment, to congregate in public places as heterosexuals did, to dress as one wanted, and so on.

One of the biggest changes of the past 25 years has been the cultural and political shift away from arguing for gay rights based on behavior to arguing for gay rights based on identity. These two concepts are, of course, intertwined, but are quite distinct. After Stonewall, we were fighting for the right to engage in homosexual acts—in short, the right to have a sex life. Now the goal has shifted: we're arguing for the right to *identify* as gay. Several months ago an appeals court in Seattle ruled that Margarethe Cammermeyer, a lesbian Air Force nurse who had been discharged because of her sexuality, had to be reinstated. The judge who issued the ruling wrote that "there is no rational basis for the Government's underlying contention that homosexual orientation equals 'desire or propensity to engage' in homosexual conduct." This ruling was terrible for two reasons: first, because it is complete nonsense; and second, because it paves the way for legal reform that would continue to penalize same-sex sexual *behavior*.

No one would argue that a heterosexual orientation would not lead to a desire or propensity to engage in heterosexual acts. And yet, this ruling is praised by the entire civil rights community! The religious Right has so stigmatized gay sexuality that, in a misguided attempt to find secure tactics in our fight, we have ceded them this crucial ground. The flight from defending behavior is apparent in the many calls from within the community to keep "fringe" groups such as drag queens and leather people at low profile in events such as the 1993 March on Washington and the

Stonewall 25 March in New York last summer. It is the constant calls for gay people to present a "good image" to the straight world. It is the new wave of books for kids of gay families, such as *Uncle What-Is-It Is Coming to Visit*, which presents non-"normal"-looking homosexuals as frightening to children. It is the "Don't ask, don't tell" policy. It is the essays of gay conservatives such as Andrew Sullivan, Bruce Bawer, and Mel White when they argue that the "good gays" are being thwarted in their political efforts by the "bad gays" who insist on talking about sex.

The construction of homosexuality without sex occurred for a number of reasons. The assimilationist trend in the movement—from homophile groups to all those looking for a place at the table—has always wanted to downplay the difficult question of sexuality. According to them, if we just never mentioned sex, we would be accepted—or at least go unnoticed. But the energy of Stonewall and the Sexual Revolution of the 1960s assumed that the concept of gay rights meant the right to be sexual, the right to act upon our sexuality in the same way that heterosexuals do.

Another reason for this shift in thinking and tactics has been the AIDS epidemic. AIDS is indisputably about behavior. Identity is not even a question here. "Gay" men are not at high risk for HIV infection; men who have sex with men are. The specter and the reality of HIV/AIDS are so overwhelming, so ingrained in the everyday lives of gay men, that on some level we simply gave up arguing for our right to behave sexually the way we wanted to. Our sexual behavior is too closely connected to HIV/AIDS to make us feel comfortable keeping it as the cornerstone of our fight for freedom.

We see this flight from behavior reflected in many mirrors. Recently an AIDS care worker, referring to a new bathhouse opening in Boston, said to me, "This is the last thing we need now." When I pointed out that the new facility was to be completely supervised, filled with safe-sex information, and supplying condoms, he responded: "I don't care This makes it look as if the only thing gay men are interested in is sex." Gay conservatives like Bruce Bawer, Hunter Madsen, and Marshall Kirk argue that the bad behavior of gay men (and that includes consuming pornography, kissing in public, marching in a Pride parade in a leather vest) stigmatizes the whole community and makes it more difficult for younger gay people to come out. Bawer's assumption in *A Place at the Table* that young people are more interested in establishing a gay identity than in having gay sex is symptomatic of this general trend.

The war on sex has escalated in the past five years. The attack on NEA funding of controversial artists is at its heart an attack on sexuality in all of its manifestations. The new Republican attack on unmarried mothers—singling them out for public scorn and chastisement—is a veiled attack on reproductive freedom. The attacks on sex education and AIDS education are an attempt to derail the progress we have made in promoting ideas of sexual freedom. When a "liberal" president fires his surgeon general because she thinks that masturbation might be a fit topic for sex education classes, you know we have reached another low point in the freedom to discuss sexuality!

Stonewall was about many things. It was about freedom of association, identity, visibility; about not being discriminated against; about not having basic human rights violated. But it was also about sex—sex without guilt, better sex, sex at home, sex at the baths, sex with or without love. If we are fighting a battle that will grant us the right to identify as gay but not the right to act accordingly, if we think we can gain acceptance by hiding the fact that our sexual desires and actions are vital aspects of our lives, we have failed completely in our struggle.

We live in a culture that both hates and obsesses about sex. And those are the heterosexuals! No wonder it's hard to talk publicly about sexuality if you are gay. We bear the burden of having to be both completely defined by our sexuality and pilloried for it at the same time. At once we are presumed to be obsessed with sex and told that only by avoiding any manifestation of it will we be accepted. In New York this past summer, it was glorious to see all those same-sex couples walking hand-in-hand—a dream not so much of "liberation" as of the relaxed possibility of simply being ourselves. But we should not rest with that dream. The harsh reality is that for the rest of the time, almost everywhere in the U.S., such seemingly inconsequential behavior simply does not and cannot occur.

We are entering a cultural space and time in which we are talking less about sexuality. Even though sex is consumerized daily—both in mainstream and in gay culture—we are no longer talking about it seriously, really talking about its importance in our lives, in our organizing, in our community building, as a major part of our identity, and as a way to secure self-respect.

AIDS and the religious Right have placed us in a state of shock about sex. But in order to come up with safe-sex campaigns that work, we're going to have to relearn how to talk about sex in a more positive language. Up until now, most safe-sex campaigns, although ostensibly "pro-sex," have adopted the approach of "Don't do this" rather than "Do that." The AIDS epidemic has exposed the fallacy of dealing with identity and not behavior. It demands that we deal directly and honestly with how we have sex, what it means to have sex, and how we can continue to have sex without killing ourselves.

We have become ashamed of our sexual desires and have allowed the religious Right, run-of-the-mill conservatives, and mere convention to dictate what we can talk about and where, what we can do with our bodies and where, and with whom. If the religious Right is going to dwell on all aspects of our sexuality—such as S/M, NAMBLA, drag, and cruising—we have to have solid, pro-gay, pro-sex answers. Simply saying "Not all gay men are drag queens" or "NAMBLA isn't about homosexuality, it's about pedophilia" isn't enough.

Until we can begin—again—to talk honestly and openly about sex and our own personal sexuality, we will never move ahead. Twenty-five years ago, the Stonewall Riots and the formation of the Gay Liberation Front were a revelation. They were not perfect, by any means, but they pointed us in the right direction. Now, a quarter of a century later, the inspirations and instincts we had then can provide us with a way to work our way through to the future.

What Became of the Spirit of '69?

Arnie Kantrowitz

IN 1970, as an officer of New York's Gay Activists Alliance, I was an enthusiastic participant in the first Gay Pride march. It was one of the best days of my entire life. Only a few hundred activists were daring enough to join in at the beginning, but our numbers swelled to around 10,000 by the time we reached Central Park. When those of us toward the front turned around and saw so many people streaming behind us, it brought tears to our eyes. Eventually we would grow to half a million (give or take a few hundred thousand).

Fractiousness was part of our movement from the beginning. Following Stonewall, gay and lesbian activists disagreed with the Homophile movement that had preceded the Riots, because it had asked merely for "tolerance" of homosexuals. In 1969, in the wake of the Civil Rights movement and a growing feminist movement, it was time to demand full equality. The Gay Liberation Front (GLF), founded immediately after Stonewall, opted for a revolutionary stance, supporting progressive leftist causes in hope of winning support from other oppressed minorities interested in forming a newly restructured society. There was a new sense of community, manifested in celebratory dances and spirited demonstrations, but political progress was not as easy. Modeling their structure on Marxist theory, the early activists met in discrete "cells" devoted to specific issues and arrived at decisions through consensus, which required laborious discussions that lasted until everyone reached agreement. Whenever a consensus was not reached, there was paralysis.

Within six months, a dozen dissatisfied members of GLF decided to split off to form the Gay Activists Alliance (GAA), a new group dedicated solely to the cause of gay rights, hoping to bring about legal reforms as well as a change of consciousness in mainstream culture. They too enjoyed a heightened sense of community spirit, which energized their huge dances and nonviolent "zaps" of public officials and institutions. However, their meetings were run according to Robert's Rules of Order, and their decisions were reached by majority vote. The system worked more effectively toward reaching specific political aims, such as the enactment of civil rights laws protecting gay jobs and homes. Still, like its parent organization, GAA was an unstable mass of constituencies with widely diverging needs and agendas.

Both organizations had high egalitarian ideals, but both attracted few people of color: only those who felt comfortable working in white-dominated groups. Both groups thought they were battling sexism, but the women of GLF split off to form Radicalesbians, and those of GAA split off to form Lesbian Feminist Liberation, leaving behind only those women who felt comfortable working in male-dominated groups. Both organizations tried to be sensitive to the needs of the other minorities within the community—the poor, the "street people," the drag queens, the leather folks—but not infrequently these groups clashed, and the largely middle-class radicals had their hands full trying to keep the peace when, for example, lesbians charged that drag queens lampooned the garments that oppressed women, or when blacks confronted the sadomasochists for playing games of "slavery." All this turmoil took place amid the exuberant sexual experimentation of the '70s. That these groups lasted as long as they did is a marvel, but by the mid-'70s the radical movement was beginning to subside.

In the meantime, a less chaotic, more enduring style of activism was being born. While some gay and lesbian activists continued to shake their fists at the bastions of established power, others had begun to take their campaign for reform inside the citadels of power. Tired of tripping over the stumbling blocks of a large grass-roots organization of activists, in 1973 several members of GAA organized the National Gay Task Force, based on the premise that a small board of efficient lobbyists could effect more change than a large fragmented organization. Other, more localized groups also formed, and soon there were lobbyists throughout the country getting state after state to enact anti-discrimination laws. Openly gay and lesbian candidates began to be appointed and elected to office around the nation. During that period, self-help groups organized services ranging from academic programs, medicine (later, AIDS support systems), legal help, and psychological counseling to professional organizations, film festivals, athletic competitions, churches, and associations based on every conceivable connection people within the community might have.

The AIDS epidemic generated a resurgence of street activism in the 1980s, first in the efforts of ACT UP (the AIDS Coalition to Unleash Power), which was, like the GAA, a single-issue organization, and later in the more gay-liberation-focused spinoff Queer Nation. Researching an article, I visited a meeting of Queer Nation and felt I had been plunged back into a GAA meeting in the early '70s, fervor, factionalism and all. Like their activist predecessors, these groups generated a great deal of light and sound, effected some changes, and then faded into history. Some organizations, like the Gay and Lesbian Alliance Against Defamation (GLAAD), of which I was a founding member, began with radical demonstrations and angry public meetings and grew into professionally staffed national groups with sophisticated Internet communications and the ability to challenge media sources for misrepresenting of our lives. Where once homosexuality was a forbidden subject in movies and called a "perversion" by respected newspapers, now there is an effort to include gay characters on the screen, who are slowly but surely changing from caricatures to ordinary people; and there is a willingness in at least the more liberal press to offer a "gay" perspective on things.

ALONG with these developments, there emerged a new, visibly affluent minority of gays that was soon courted by the likes of travel agents, liquor companies, clothing designers, furniture outlets, gyms, and all the other seductions of consumerism. Once the revolutionary fervor subsided, the effort at reform brought with it a drive toward normalization. Rather than attempt to alter the course of mainstream culture, there was an eagerness to join its flow. Where gays once protested the military's wars, they would eventually press for the right to serve in the armed services. Where once our strategists spoke of overthrowing the state's regulation of monogamy and glorified the freedoms of promiscuity, today same-sex couples register as domestic partners with attendant insurance and inheritance benefits and sue for the right to legally sanctioned marriage and the right to adopt children. Where once gays demonstrated against the homophobia of churches, now they seek full equality on both sides of the pulpit. I don't recall many gay Republicans back in the '70s, but now we have a national gay organization dedicated to the party of Nixon. Meanwhile, the Human Rights Campaign has been addressed by an incumbent president, even as its subsequent endorsements shocked its own members for their conservatism, and the HRC-sponsored March on Washington 2000 is expected to pay homage to "Faith and Family." What a long way we have traveled in thirty years!

The concept of gay pride is still in its historical childhood, but although we never had time to experience it fully before we were suddenly swept up in the winds of pestilence, its critics are already beginning to declare it dead. The virulence with which the gay generation is being reviled by its offspring is startling. The gay activists of the '70s dared to proclaim their homosexuality publicly and confront their heterosexual oppressors while considering bisexuality a timid refusal to come all the way out of the closet. Today's "queer theorists" are challenging the rigid categories of "gay" and "straight," maintaining that each individual's sexual identity is malleable over time. In books like Michelangelo Signorile's *Life Outside*, young social commentators of the next generation are attacking the narcissistic values of the culture spawned by gay society. Same-sex novelist John Weir, in Mark Simpson's anthology *Anti-Gay*, sides with the homophobes: "I'm sick of gay men. The next time I see a bunch of dudes from Jersey beating on a faggot from Greenwich Village, I'm going to cheer them on."

Daniel Harris in *The Rise and Fall of Gay Culture* puts "gay" in the past tense, maintaining that our battles are basically won and there is little in store for us save mainstream consumerism. Conservative Bruce Bawer wants us to have "a place at the table"—regardless of what repression is being served. AIDS activists like Gabriel Rotello (*Sexual Ecology*) are questioning the wisdom of the gay sexual revolution and calling for a hetero-imitative refashioning of male love in order to stop a resurgence of the epidemic. Andrew Sullivan argues in *Virtually Normal* that once we've won the right to marry and serve in the military, our battle is essentially done. Writers like Douglas Sadownick (in *Sex Between Men*) offer respect for the '70s freedom of spirit, but even some of my contemporaries, like Ian Young in *The Stonewall Experiment*, are reassessing the '70s and recasting them as a time of deluded desperation. Recently the term "post-gay" surfaced briefly to declare a chic distaste for gay Pride parades with their lambdas, pink triangles, and rainbow flags, along with the promiscuity and consumerism with which they have been associated.

The perspective from which we evaluate our experience is shaped by the landscape that greets us when first we come to awareness. The revolution of the 1970s was a refreshing change from the guilt and repression of the previous decades. Dressing like "clones" not only proclaimed our solidarity in public, it liberated our maleness (including public announcement of our specific sexual preferences with a rainbow of colored bandannas sprouting jauntily from our rear pockets). We went to gay clubs and gyms, ate in gay restaurants, vacationed at gay resorts, shopped in newly created gay stores, wrote and read gay books and magazines in increasing numbers. Even if we had to be more careful only a few blocks from Christopher Street, we didn't see our neighborhood as a prison. We saw it as the promised land; we were at the cutting edge of politics and sociology and (of course) fashion; we were "sexual pioneers"—and I for one was having the time of my life!

My generation attacked the "homophile" generation for not demanding enough, for accepting second-class status as long as gays were treated with compassion. Now the "queer" generation—in a similar Oedipal struggle to assert its own identity—seems to be attacking the "gay and lesbian" generation for demanding too much. In their eyes. we constructed a sand castle built on a foundation of hedonism and "identity politics." This combination led to the commercialization of our values, a narcissistic commitment to personal image, and, in short, to the failure of the revolution. They have a good point. Their idea of liberation follows from the more general lowering of expectations in American society with respect to social change; it is difficult for people coming of age in the '90s to understand the idealism of the '60s and '70s. We could stop wars, create social justice, overcome all oppressors. Young people today resent their parents' enthusiasm, branding it as naïve. Those who have no memory of pre-Stonewall oppression take for granted the gains won by my generation.

What will happen over the next decades of our struggle? My expectation is that the model of gays and lesbians will become normalized, hardly distinguishable from the rest of America's homogenized citizenry. Despite the dogged resistance of the religious Right, and barring a total fascist takeover, I believe we will win the right to marry and to serve in the military. Some of us still do not want these rights, but it's probably too late to stop what we've set in motion. We gay and lesbian sexual revolutionaries of the '70s thought that we would change America by demanding inclusion, but America's means of including outsiders has always been to change *them*. Every group that has preceded us into the mainstream has had to sacrifice whatever it held dearest, that which made it different and special—its distinctive faith, its ethnic customs, its political radicalism, its sexual libertinism. This unintended prize of our revolution may be far from our original dream, but no dream remains unchanged when it is transformed into reality.

In the early 1970s, I wrote a piece for *The Village Voice* titled "A Gay Struggles with the New Acceptance," which said that as we revealed ourselves to the world, we could already see tourists peering into the windows of our bars on Christopher Street. The magic pink bubble that had isolated us in our own private hothouse had begun to evaporate. What's clearer now is that without that barrier, we will inevitably lose the defining line between us and the rest of society, and with it our unique identity. So now that America has seen drag queens and leather sex, women kissing and men holding hands on national TV, our fairy dust must begin to fade into history. It was a process that began before I arrived on the scene, and one that will continue far past my time. But I was there for the most magical moment of all, the moment when the closet was first unlocked.

Now I stand on the sidelines and watch the gay pride parade go by, happily greeting the occasional old-timer who's still marching. I hope the younger generation has as good a time as we did, and wherever history takes us, I hope they and those who come after them will look back on our era and see that, despite its faults, gay liberation was a critical rung on our ladder to full equality.

At Thirty Years A.S. (After Stonewall)

DENNIS ALTMAN

I ARRIVED in New York from Australia in 1970, a year after Stonewall, to find a radical gay community in the making, one that quickly became my political home. I took up residence with a painter, Adolph Garcia, on the edge of the East Village. Adolph lived in a sprawling seven-room apartment on Second Avenue, decorated with his paintings of shoes, and made the apartment available for meetings of the new gay liberation paper, *Come Out*. I gravitated to the burgeoning network of radical gay groups forming in New York, writing for the paper and attending interminable meetings, which were exciting and welcome because they offered a kind of community that I had not yet experienced in the commercial world of bars and saunas. Gay women and men—the word gay was used inclusively then—had been radicalized by the Civil Rights movement, the antiwar movement, and a reborn feminist movement, and gay politics was a natural progression from these struggles.

The previous year, the Stonewall Riots had led to the founding of the New York Gay Liberation Front and the emergence of the slogan "Gay Power." The excitement of this period was reflected in my first book, *Homosexual: Oppression and Liberation*, which grew out of my experiences of New York over the winter and spring of 1970-71. That book recounted in some detail the politics and discoveries of the first several years of gay liberation. It also reflected the enormous influence on my generation of gay writers such as James Baldwin and Christopher Isherwood, and a number of social theorists, notably Herbert Marcuse, who had fled Germany for the U.S. in the 1930s, and whose attempt to synthesize Marxism and psychoanalysis in *Eros and Civilization* became a cult must-read in the late 1960s and early '70s. It was through Marcuse that I came to Freud, almost by accident, and it wasn't until after completing the book that I read his writings systematically. Like some of the European gay liberation theorists—but unlike American gay activists—I found in Freud a radical defense of sexual diversity, a plea both for acceptance of human variety and of human weakness. This has not been a popular position in the Anglo-American gay world, which has tended to assume that psychoanalysis was part of the normalizing apparatus of homophobia.

Freud's concept of "polymorphous perversity," the notion that there's a human potential for enormous fluidity of sexual desires, which I found quite appealing, was anathema to a movement that was increasingly insisting upon a fixed dichotomy between "gay" and "straight." Only in the last decade have "queer" attacks on identity politics revived a belief in the fluidity of sexuality, though often without any apparent awareness of the origins of these ideas in Freud.

Ironically enough, the book was given wide publicity by a review in *Time* that was by no means flattering. "The chest-thumping insistence that homosexual love is just like (and exactly as desirable as) heterosexual love," the reviewer wrote, "is self-defeating. It is also biologically inaccurate and socially unsound." But even a *bad* review in *Time* magazine can sell books, and this recognition gave the book an enormous boost. My next two books—a collection of essays, *Coming Out in the Seventies* (1979), and *The Homosexualization of America* (1982)—were both in a sense sequels to the first.

The contemporary lesbigay movement [in 1999] was born in the years after Stonewall, when a whole set of social, cultural and political movements seemed to promise a new society. Odd as it may seem now, the possibility of revolutionary change appeared real to people as divergent as President Nixon and the Black Panthers. Of the movement's goals Jonathan Ned Katz wrote: "In that heady, hopeful, exhilarating dawn of gay and lesbian liberation, the abolition of heterosexuality and the end of homosexuality were in the air. We dared to imagine a radically free and different sexual future." Katz' idea of abolishing the sexual categories foreshadows some of the ideas of queer theory in the 1990s. That the "queer" concept presented itself as a critique of today's "mainstream" movement underscores the radicalism of the early movement's outlook and objectives.

Perhaps the most important development was the growth of a commercial sector around gay and (to a lesser extent) lesbian world. Bars, saunas, and restaurants proliferated, joined by a plethora of gay publications (*The Advocate, Body Politics,* and *GCN* being the most important ones in the '70s). New institutions such as the Metropolitan Community Church and the Gay Games legitimized new ways of being lesbian and gay—and spread to thousands of people outside the U.S. Gradually being gay or lesbian came to be something one could integrate with the rest of one's life, rather than a dirty secret that had to be protected from public disclosure (even if many remnants of the latter attitude remain in force to this day).

"Do you rescind anything in *Homosexual*?" I was asked recently by someone deliberately echoing that favorite malapropism of politicians. Allowing for the rhetorical excesses of the early '70s, I'd have to say that the answer is No, and that I'm somewhat surprised at the extent to which this book—and more importantly the political world it reflected—set a framework that's still relevant today. While the gay liberation movement itself is fading into memory, it did succeed in raising almost all of the large questions with which we're still struggling, above all the central dilemma of how both to create a homosexual community and to assert the right to be fully integrated into the larger civil society. In those early days we knew intuitively, I think, that there was a tension between wanting to build gay / lesbian community and seeking full equality as citizens. It was the same sort of tension that all oppressed groups have faced in defining themselves in relation to the majority. We also knew that homosexuality touched on a range of taboos around sex and gender, even if we lacked the subtlety—and the jargon—of people like Eve Kosofsky Sedgwick and Judith Butler.

At the time, we thought we were the political radicals and scorned those whose focus was on decriminalization and legal change. We assumed, in the dominant Leftist ideology of the time, that gay liberation was both part of and depended upon larger social change. What we failed to foresee was that Western societies could become more economically unequal *and* more socially liberal at the same time. I don't think any of us foresaw how advertisers and Hollywood would come to chase the "lavender dollar." For in the end it is capitalism, not moral arguments, that rendered homophobia old-fashioned and unacceptable.

In *Homosexual* I had written: "Gay liberation is part of a much wider movement that's challenging the basic cultural norms of our advanced capitalist, industrial and bureaucratic society, and bringing about changes in individual consciousness and new identities and lifestyles." We don't much talk in this language anymore, but there is an echo of such talk in some of today's politics around indigenous and multicultural lesbigay groups, and, for all the postmodern blurring of terms, what can still be recognized as a voice from the Left.

The gay and lesbian movement has had extraordinary achievements in the past decade or two, ranging from the creation of an extensive community-based response to AIDS to the successful use of international human rights institutions to overturn sodomy laws in a number of countries (though not yet in the U.S. [until 2003 with *Lawrence v. Texas*]). Openly lesbian and gay politicians have been elected to a number of Western legislatures; some countries (and in South Africa the Constitution itself) include us among their protected categories in anti-discrimination laws. Much remains to be done, but the rate of change has been faster than we might have predicted 25 years ago. On an international scale, the inability of the U.S. to scrap its sodomy laws remains a bizarre anomaly, equivalent to the American commitment to capital punishment—both of them linked to the peculiar religiosity of American society.

It is currently fashionable to question the reality of fixed sexual identities and to deconstruct the concept of a community based on sexual orientation. Rather than question their authenticity, in my view, we might better spend our energies examining the sorts of communities we have created. To what extent, for example, are we replicating within our own communities the sexism, racism, and class structures of the broader society? To do this requires more knowledge of the history of our movement than the contemporary vogue for theory and deconstruction allows. One of the great paradoxes of much contemporary queer writing is the way in which it removes the concrete actors whose hard work is what made institutions like Pride parades possible at all.

Sex, Pride, and Desire

FRANK BROWNING

DISSIDENT desires win tolerance and respect in America only after they have been rendered and processed into the language of politics, law, and commerce. The subtle, shifting force of desire itself is seldom defended except in spiritual terms. Homosexual sex—indeed sex at all—remains untouchable territory for public discourse. We can use its dressing, its symbols, to sell blue jeans, power drills, and Chevies, but the thing itself remains oddly embarrassing even in the flourishing gay press. Nowhere in the major gay magazines do we read writing that dares to be as psychologically rich and sexually evocative as Jean Genet or Marcel Proust or even D. H. Lawrence. Instead, the gay media publish heroic or disturbing stories about marriage, career, adoption, entertainment, health, and business—the public benchmarks of an emerging social constituency. These are, of course, valuable stories, and I have written or reported on radio for my share of them. Even so, none of these stories would have any meaning at all, the narratives could not even exist, but for the rumbling dissidence of desire.

Desire, however, scares us. As much as they were driven by their own sexual appetites, the often heroic men and women who made the movement powerful have understood that the shadowy, psychological labyrinths of human desire cannot be directly discussed in America—any more than the appetites of Bill Clinton, Pamela Harriman, or Jack Kennedy could be acknowledged so long as they wished to be politically effective. Ours is a culture—and has been since its founding—that requires not merely the sublimation of desire (which of the Judeo-Christian societies do not?) but the active, concentrated suppression of public discussion of sex (of which the persistent Congressional prohibition against funding safe-sex instruction or the dismissal of Surgeon General Joycelyn

Elders after mentioning masturbation are clear examples).

By desire I do not mean floodlit descriptions of sex acts. Instead, I mean the demons, the shibboleths, the fantasies, the dreams, that carry us hungrily toward the flesh of another human. In the vital political campaign for "rights," in the personal campaigns for "pride" and self-improvement, we have, I fear, discarded the wondrous and terrible embattlements of desire—the very stuff of Æschylus or Shakespeare or O'Neill or Capote—for a promotional politics of public respect. That may be necessary, for us, in America. Andrew Sullivan, the Tory revisionist, has argued persuasively that in a modern society, the only legitimate political movements are those that seek to remove state barriers to private acts. Æsthetic, psychological, and cultural concerns should be excluded from political discourse lest all art degenerate to the vulgar standards of the majority. Sullivan, as well as war horse activists like Larry Kramer and David Mixner or younger "zapsters" like Michelangelo Signorile, seem to share with the major gay rights organizations the belief that public discourse should restrict itself to the legal and economic interests of identifiable actors and groups.

The liberationist and transformational objectives of the early gay movement, and even the brief "queer" cultural insurgency of the late "80s and early '90s, have dissipated. The pursuit of sexual pleasure as a legitimate social concern has disappeared from the movement's public agenda. In its place have come the right to participate in war, the right to marry, the right to adopt children, and so on. Front-line gay activists rally for the sacredness of the homosexual while dismissing sexual desire. Rather than press the society to enlarge and enrich its sexual culture, they argue, agitate, and seek to legislate for the rights and interests of gay people as any other identity group.

In effect, the gay movement has adopted the social and legal strategy worked out by the racial and ethnic minorities that have eventually found a voice in the American story—such as the Irish in Boston, the Jews in New York, the Italians in Chicago, the Chinese in San Francisco, or the Japanese in L.A. It is a model with a proven history. More to the point, gay men and lesbians of my (forty-plus) generation, as well as dissident young queers, have benefited enormously from this most American of strategies. That is why those of us in mid-life, especially those of us who are finally accumulating the social accouterments of respect, grow so upset at any incipient challenge to the sanctity of gay identity. Gay Pride, surely the movement's most cherished slogan, rests on the idea of a group identity.

The adoption of "Pride" as the gay slogan of choice displays how fundamentally *American* this movement really is. Merged with pink triangles and rainbow flags, Pride has become America's global gay export. Other cultures have fought to remove oppressive laws, to defend homoeroticism in art and literature, even to build gay bohemian enclaves. But it took the land of 10,000 self-help manuals, the nation where pop psychologists convinced legislators that "self-esteem" is a legitimate public policy objective, to elevate pride into a civil rights campaign. Pride as the alternative to shame carries a simple, common-sense utility in a society that regards certain people as less than fully human. That has been true for both black people and gay people in this century. But reciting the word repeatedly bears a cost. Pride itself has no necessary political meaning. It tells us nothing about what we want from life, and, as the Greeks understood 3,000 years ago, pride tends eventually toward inward self-absorption. Seldom do the self-absorbed see the peculiarity of their own position, and almost never do they recognize and respect others who hold different values, display different behaviors, or understand their sexuality in different terms.

WHEN I first began the work that lead to *The Culture of Desire,* I had a central question in mind: had the social movement born among homosexual men in the 1960s and '70s succeeded in creating a distinct culture that would meet the first fundamental requirement of any culture, namely, that it regenerate itself in recognizable form through successive generations? Did gay culture exist? Was it anything more than a temporary media and marketing phenomenon drawn together in response to sexual fear and bigotry?

Today I am less certain of the reality of gay life than I have ever been. Nothing has made that uncertainty stand out more sharply than the debates over marriage, sex, and the military that have swept over gay discourse in the '90s. On the one hand, the carefully orchestrated campaigns for opening both marriage and the military to out gay people has been conducted along classic civil rights lines. Seen as a call for equal access to the rights and institutions provided all citizens, the campaigns are surely unassailable. Never should a constitutional democracy erect arbitrary exclusions based on the status of any of its citizens. As Andrew Sullivan has argued cogently in two books and numerous public appearances, nothing would more effectively counter the demonization of homosexuals—and thereby normalize them—than to remove these particular barriers. Richard Isay, the gay psychotherapist, made a parallel argument in the late 1980s when he wrote that it was the very unavailability of marriage that encouraged so much of the sexual adventuring of gay men. Make marriage available, he argued, and we would likely settle down into responsible domesticated households.

In the spring of 1998, two former promoters turned queer activists turned respectable journalists published two books calling variously for just such a reformulation of what it means to be gay and male. Gabriel Rotello's *Sexual Ecology* recapitulated what epidemiologists had said since the early days of the AIDS epidemic: sharp rises in the number of sexual contacts men have with each other will increase the rate of HIV transmission as well as traditional venereal diseases like gonorrhea, genital herpes, and chlamydia. Michelangelo Signorile, whose early "outing" stories Rotello had edited at the feisty New York weekly *OutWeek*, published a book that surveyed the fast-track urban ghetto scene of bars, gyms, steroids, designer drugs, and the movable sex rodeos called circuit parties, and found it all vapid. Together, Rotello and Signorile issued a clarion call for a radical reversal of the middle-class gay project. A culture that celebrated sexual play—recreational sex—as an end in itself was flawed at its foundation and doomed to a fate of disease, banality, and empty indulgence. "What kinds of rewards might encourage gay men to adopt a culture of sexual restraint and responsibility, one in which they will be likely to reduce their contact rate and be as safe as possible within relationships?" Rotello asked. "It seems likely that they are the same rewards that influence most people: a culture that grants status to those who exercise restraint and responsibility, and by implication withholds status from those who don't."

Larry Kramer, the one-time screenwriter turned heroic AIDS activist turned self-important tantrum artist, took their cause several steps further: the gay literary estate itself, of which he had never been considered a particularly talented member, was drenched in blood and should be driven from the pantheon, shamed for its promotion of wanton sexuality. Kramer, best known for denouncing famed AIDS researcher Dr. Anthony Fauci as an assassin, has long favored hyperbole over insight (dismissing his comrades at Gay Men's Health Crisis and ACT UP as cowards and quislings), but his attack on gay literature did help to crystallize one of the central contradictions in modern gay life: If sex is not the central defining force in homosexual experience, then what is? And if our sexual passions are our only distinctive bond, do we not set ourselves up as perpetual outsiders, reduced by physical appetite to a culture of cartoon libidos? Do we not feel love beyond lust, Kramer, Rotello, and Signorile ask? Have we no ambition elsewhere in the world? Do we not dare to erect great cathedrals, engineer fine bridges, rebuild the cities, negotiate peace accords? Do we not care to keep house and raise children?

Those of us who embrace the liberating power of sex and other sins of pleasure are foolish and dishonest if we deny the destructive power that is inseparable from the pursuit of the sublime. No sex is without risk—of callousness, of aloofness, of abuse, and of disease. Equally, we are blind to ignore the vacuous banality of the relentless chase after bar boys and gym bodies that underwrites the commercial base of contemporary gay life in America. Rotello and Signorile have tapped into a genuine angst as they face a midlife in which house music and locker rooms have ceased to reward them or to provide any sense of human satisfaction.

What these writers somehow seem to have missed is that gay people do not live in some hermetically insulated world of their own invention. To suppose that the discontents of gay life are to be understood solely as an artifact of gay experience is to suffer the analytical myopia that almost always marks the partisans of identity politics. The culture of consumerized body marketing, the anomie and insularity of urban and suburban life, the desperate search for solace through style, has become the universal lament of a society that whines relentlessly about how it has been betrayed by modernism. We demand the freedom of 24-hour digital access to all the products and services of the waking world and then complain that we have no time to make our families real. We shop through all the closets and pantries of the world's people, wrap ourselves in their fabrics and dine on their delicacies but discover that we are incapable of speaking to them in any language but our own. We establish human rights watches to denounce state suppression of sexual freedom, promise the victims succor and defense on our shores, and then, as the price of their salvation, we demand that they redesign their desire to fit the identity package we invented for ourselves. Hungry for an identity of our own—any identity—we find ourselves unsatisfied by the packages we manufacture and market to each other.

PAUL Russell's 1995 compendium, *The Gay 100: A Ranking of the Most Influential Gay Men and Lesbians, Past and Present,* includes: Socrates, Alexander the Great, Michelangelo, Hadrian, Johann Winckelmann, Tchaikovsky, André Gide, Byron, Rimbaud, and Allen Ginsberg. Whether "gay" is a term that has any meaning in describing the lives they led is surely questionable, even for Allen Ginsberg. More to the point, all of these men would be considered felons by nearly all major American gay leaders today because they were, by contemporary American standards, pederasts. Many if not all their lovers were adolescents, and most wrote or spoke about them. Today, the gay consensus—as well as federal law—suggests that such men suffer a mental disease that must be treated by medicine and suppressed by the state. Each year state and federal prosecutors indict thousands of men on either child abuse or child pornography charges for having sex with males under age eighteen or purchasing photographs purportedly of under-age males. Many of these men are indeed child abusers who should be prosecuted; many, however, are not, for inter-generational love remains as real at the end of the millennium as it was in the time of Antony and Cleopatra. Such men, however, are not, according to gay orthodoxy, truly "gay," and the relationships they have had would certainly not be thought suitable for matrimony by the gay marriage advocates—which leads to a second critical question: what should we want of a marriage?

Divorce, spousal battery, and child abuse are hardly new events in family life. The dissolution of families even when they are protected by marriage has proven deeply disturbing to the entire society. The modern nuclear family based on two working parents who spend no more than two or three evenings together with their children, who themselves disappear by age eighteen has proven an increasingly barren institution, neither terribly effective at child rearing nor care for the elderly. Whatever symbolic and legal advantages the marriage contract may confer on those who would make a family, surely only the blind, deaf, and insensate can be unaware of the frail status of the conventional modern family.

Those of us who yearn for the sanction of marriage, who imagine in its contracted monogamy a balm for the emptiness and banality of the circuit, will probably find ourselves in line for the disappointments that always accompany nostalgic naïveté. Pederasts or peers, our most attractive longings are for solidarity, fulfillment, and love. That said, peers and pederasts alike are also motivated by insecurity, ambition, and the will to dominate—as a week spent in divorce court will easily reveal. Marriage itself guarantees no particular blend of our darker and brighter motivations, but the substitution of marriage campaigns for a collective inquiry into our genuine family needs seems likely to produce little more than a gay shadow of the mindless "family values" shibboleths already flooding the airwaves. Compounded with a boilerplate code of sexual conduct based on the panic of middle age and a nostalgic longing for simplistic solutions, these new preachers of sexual reform promise anything but a progressive civil rights agenda. Their movement seeks, as nearly all identity politics movements eventually do, to police rather than to liberate, to supplant reaction for comprehension, to turn inward toward the security of convention rather than outward toward the complexities of human desire. Theirs is, indeed, a queer movement, but it takes as its ultimate target the soul of genuine queerness.

The Quest for Identity

AMY HOFFMAN

RECOVERING or reframing history—creating a "people's history"—has been important for all identity-based social movements, but it's been crucial and particularly revelatory for the GLBT movement. Michel Foucault says, as quoted in Eve Sedgwick's *Epistemology of the Closet* (1990): "There is no binary division to be made between what one says and what one does not say; we must try to determine the different ways of not saying things. ... There is not one but many silences, and they are an integral part of the strategies that underlie and permeate discourses." What he means, I think, is that silence itself communicates specific, complex social messages, for a variety of reasons. We had a nice example of this recently when the reporter Anderson Cooper came out in a statement to blogger Andrew Sullivan. The curious thing about Cooper's statement was that it was already widely known that he's gay. Even I knew it, and I rarely watch TV news and know almost nothing else about him. The media eagerly covered Cooper's statement while paradoxically maintaining that it was not much of a story—which *The New York Times* business section, for one, hailed as a sign of today's acceptance of gay men and lesbians in the media.

In a perceptive op-ed commentary in the *Times* (July 3, 2012) a few days after Cooper's non-revelation, the gay author and essayist Daniel Mendelsohn noted that "gay celebrities enjoy the protection of a cozy *omertà* among the social and media circles like the one that shielded Mr. Cooper." Interestingly, Mendelsohn continued, this code enabled Cooper to deny that he was ever closeted: "'I have always been very open and honest about this part of my life with my friends, my family, and my colleagues,' he wrote to Mr. Sullivan. 'In a perfect world, I don't think it's anyone else's business.'" This is getting complicated: if it's nobody's business, then why the need to be "open and honest"? And how out must you be to be truly "out"? If Cooper wasn't out to his media audience, was he indeed being "open and honest"? Mendelsohn points out that Cooper wrote a book in which he discussed other personal issues—but not his sexuality. He goes on to say: "The high-minded appeal to privacy is, indeed, now a trope in the coming-out process of public figures and celebrities...[But] if you're really 'happy, comfortable ... and proud' to be gay, as Mr. Cooper says he is, the simple fact of being gay should be no more a 'privacy' issue than being straight is for straight people."

In a recent essay collection *The Fan Who Knew Too Much* (2012), the gospel historian Anthony Heilbut points to another instance of this sort of "out but not out" status: black gay men in the black church who, Heilbut maintains, are the sources, as singers, musicians, and dancers, of the church's very "spirit" and "soul." These men are far from the elite, but, as with Cooper, their sexuality is an open secret, so much so that there's a name for it: gay men in the church are called "the children." Writes Heilbut:

> The church and its gospel music have offered a second home, and often a friendlier place than the homes where boys might face ridicule or worse. ... Gospel has allowed the worship of a loving male. ... I have seen five-man groups weep and stagger as they sang "When sorrow has taken my heart by surprise, He never has left me alone." ... They'll wave glad hands when some old mother exhorts them, "Children, take it to Jesus, you don't need to tell nobody else. Just step into your secret closet."

(This is a reference, says Heilbut, to Matthew 6:6: "But thou, when thou prayest, enter into thy closet, and when thou hast shut thy door, pray to thy Father which is in secret; and thy Father which seeth in secret shall reward thee openly.") James Baldwin's wonderful final novel, *Just Above My Head* (1979), is about just such a black gay gospel singer—and for this reason (I believe) was dissed by critics when it was first published.

So what is the meaning of this particular silence—about something that, as the singer Leonard Cohen would say, "everybody knows"? Oscar Wilde's lover Lord Alfred Douglas famously called homosexuality "the love that dare not speak its name." And as any kid worrying about whether and how and when to come out to his or her family can tell you, there's a big difference between everyone knowing you're gay, and telling them you're gay. A cousin of mine, whom my brother used to call the pink sheep of the family, begged me, when he (rather unnecessarily) came out to me, not to tell his grandmother, my great aunt. She, like everyone else in the family, knew of course that he was gay—but to tell her he was gay would have been to risk their loving relationship. The problem is not being gay; it's breaking the silence, acknowledging it, forcing it into the discussion.

GLBT folk history has it that the 1885 Labouchere Amendment, which basically banned male homosexual acts in the UK and was not repealed until 1967, did not include lesbianism because Queen Victoria denied the possibility that women would or could engage in such behavior. According to many historians, most influentially Carol Smith-Rosenberg in her groundbreaking 1975 essay in *Signs*, "The Female World of Love and Ritual," Victorian women's letters and diaries show that they did form deep, loving, lifelong relationships that were often more important to them than their marriages. They were physically affectionate and even slept together, though it's not clear if they had what we'd define as sex or thought of their relationships as sexual.

The lesbian historian Lillian Faderman, in her 1981 book *Surpassing the Love of Men*, comes close to arguing that it was sexologists like Havelock Ellis and Sigmund Freud who ruined everything by labeling such unions as homosexual and making it impossible for women to remain innocent of the sexual component of their relationships. Before Freud, Faderman says, the relationships were seen as healthy and normal. "The sexologists' theories frightened, or attempted to frighten, women away from feminism and from loving other women by demonstrating that both were abnormal and were generally linked together," she writes of the sexologists' influence. "In America, it took the phenomenal growth of female autonomy during and after World War I, and the American popularization of the most influential of the European sexologists, Sigmund Freud, to cast the widespread suspicions on love between women that had already been prevalent in Europe."

OUR laundry-list name for our movement—GLBT—to which some add "QQI" for Queer, Questioning, and Intersex—demonstrates that we are still struggling with definitions and identity. Who are we, anyway? And how can we find out? At the outset of the movement, after the Stonewall Riots in Greenwich Village in June 1969, we didn't have much history—because we didn't have the language in which to communicate it, to speak about our experience, our knowledge, our selves. When there were no images of GLBT people—no definitions, no words, no stories, no Ellen DeGeneres—you came out into a void. I mean, I'm Jewish. In my family, we had Jewish friends, we ate Jewish food, we sang Jewish songs, we celebrated Jewish holidays, we used Jewish words. We studied Jewish history: from the patriarchs to the Holocaust to the land of Israel. My parents taught me right from the start, never deny that you're Jewish. It's not like that if you're gay. Nobody says to you, "My sweet little lesbian—let me tell you a bedtime story about our Mother Sappho." They surely don't say, "Never deny it."

If the essential first act was to look up "homosexual" in the dictionary, the quintessential first reaction was, "I thought I was the only one!" For some, even a definition of "pervert" was a comfort. At least you belonged to a category; you weren't some kind of monstrous biological sport. This is one reason why the late Vito Russo's 1981 book, *The Celluloid Closet: Homosexuality in the Movies*, caused such a sensation among us: even if Hollywood showed us as silly, isolated, self-destructive, and violent, it affirmed our existence as recognizable types. In 1980, there were GLBT protests around the country of the film *Cruising*, by William Friedkin, a story of a gay killer of gay men starring Al Pacino. My friend Michael Bronski, the film buff and historian, claims that after the protests, he and other gay men would sneak in to watch the movie—because it showed gay men in the leather bars of Greenwich Village, and they'd never before seen themselves depicted onscreen.

But there's a paradox about the experience of seeing yourself reflected in the media. On the one hand, as I've mentioned, the media can be affirming, a demonstration that you have a definition, a social role, "reality"—a layered concept in GLBT culture. In Jennie Livingston's 1990 documentary *Paris Is Burning*, about drag competitions among gay men of color in New York City, participants are judged on "realness," which was about their skill in performing a certain gender role—which according to the philosopher Judith Butler is what gender is all about anyway. Butler says, in her usual complex language: "[G]ender is in no way a stable identity or locus of agency from which various acts proceed; rather, it is an identity tenuously constituted in time—an identity, instituted through a stylized repetition of acts. Further, gender is instituted through the stylization of the body and, hence, must be understood as the mundane way in which bodily gestures, movements, and enactments of various kinds constitute the illusion of an abiding gendered self" (*Theatre Journal*, Dec. 1988).

IN 1976, Jonathan Ned Katz published *Gay American History*, an invaluable collection of primary source documents about same-sex loving people in North America from colonial times to the present. In 1979, Allan Bérubé of the San Francisco Gay History Project toured the U.S. with the project's slideshow about those he called "passing women"—19th-century San Francisco women who dressed and lived as men. Some had married women. We would probably call them transgender now. Bérubé discovered accounts of these women in newspapers and other sources, including *Gay American History*. They ended up in the news when their sex was revealed, often when they became sick or died. It's hard for me to convey to you how thrilling it was to see Bérubé's slideshow when he brought it to Boston. Although I could recite a list of "famous gays," to a young lesbian like me it nevertheless felt as though my generation of out, politicized women—"dykes to watch out for," as cartoonist Alison Bechdel called us—was a new phenomenon.

Since GLBT history, unlike the histories of other subcultural groups, could not be passed down from generation to generation, we had to keep rediscovering it. As thrilling as it was to hear of Bérubé's miners and factory workers, it was even more exciting to learn about the women who'd come up just before us, such as the New York bar girls described in Ann Bannon's 1950s pulp novel series "The Beebo Brinker Chronicles." Beebo herself was a handsome butch who dressed in suits on her nights out and worked as an elevator operator during the day—partly because the job allowed her to wear pants. Joan Nestle, one of the founders of New York's Lesbian Herstory Archives, which for years was housed in her apartment, gave a lecture in Boston in the mid-1980s on the femmes and butches of the 1950s lesbian bars, and how she wore a black lace slip that clearly identified her as femme. She admonished us young people to stop disrespecting our foremothers—and this is an impression that many older lesbians had of the feminist lesbians of my generation. I don't think it's quite right—we didn't disdain them or their unique culture; we were simply ignorant. And indeed how could we have been anything else? Pulp fiction like the Beebo Brinker books, lesbian publications like *The Ladder*—these were hidden deep underground.

As much fun and as fulfilling as "famous gays" was, though, it eventually became apparent that it was not accurate. Just as feminists were realizing that, as Simone de Beauvoir famously put it, "One is not born but rather becomes a woman," GLBT liberationists were coming to understand that simply having gay sex (whatever that means) doesn't make you gay. (Gore Vidal maintained this about himself to the last: he insisted that he was, in his personal terminology, a "homosexualist," but not a homosexual.) In some cultures or historical periods, it was something people did at a certain stage of life, or under certain circumstances. And there were extremely varied cultural opinions about it: the ancient Greeks, for example, thought of sex between a man and a youth as beautiful and a useful pedagogical tool. In the U.S. in 2012, pedophilia can get you locked away for life. In the West, homosexual sex evolved, roughly, from being treated as a sin, to a crime, to a mental illness. In all these formulations, though, it was seen as a behavior, not an identity: something you *did*, not something you *were*. Homosexuality as an identity, a defining desire, was something that began to develop relatively recently, starting around the end of the 19th century.

Similar to the incremental "becoming" that Simone de Beauvoir posited for gender, GLBT identities grew both more established and more complex throughout the 20th and now the 21st century. Studies by history projects and individual historians have documented GLBT subcultures in U.S. cities from San Francisco to Buffalo, New York. We may be approaching a new turn in this evolution. In the introduction to St. Sukie de la Croix' new book, *Chicago Whispers: A History of GLBT Chicago Before Stonewall*, historian John D'Emilio writes this:

> In the nineteenth century, doctors wrote about gender, or sexual "inversion": men and women behaving as if they were the other gender. Eventually, they came to understand that this was "really" homosexuality—love for, and sexual attraction to, members of the same sex. As the twentieth century wore on, a self-conscious gay and lesbian community emerged. Implicit in this—and

> sometimes articulated in the rhetoric of political activists—was the sense that "gay" and "lesbian" was the real thing, while "drag" and transsexuality was a form of false consciousness, a reflection of internalized homophobia. In the last two decades, transgender activists have vigorously challenged these presuppositions, and transgender historical research has emerged. .... Reading *Chicago Whispers*, I found it hard not to notice how pervasive gender-crossing has been. It stretches across the time span covered by the book. It exists on stage and on the streets, in public and in private, as drama and as comedy, as a form of mocking social norms and as a means of finding one's true self. It is both individual and collective. It is something that individuals can turn on and off, and something that simply is. Gender crossing—as social role and as identity—seems more encompassing and enduring than homosexuality. Is it possible, I wonder, that fifty years from now, the reigning wisdom will argue that gay and lesbian proved to be relatively short blips on the historical screen and that transgender—or what I am referring to as gender crossing—provides the more robust framework for historical understanding?

D'Emilio sees the "Q" for "queer" in LGBTQ as the item in the list that will, in the end, be the most encompassing and useful definition, identity, and frame for history.

Queer Theory's Heist of Our History

LARRY KRAMER

I DO not understand why historians and academics, including many gay ones, refuse to believe that homosexuality has been pretty much the same since the beginning of human history, whether it was called homosexuality, sodomy, buggery, or had no name at all. Isn't it time for us to put a stop to this nonsense that produces retrograde books like a recent one by Richard Godbeer titled *The Overflowing of Friendship: Love between Men and the Creation of the American Republic* (Johns Hopkins University Press, 2009), another in the long line of what I call the Doris Kearns Goodwin School of History as Highway Robbery.*

Gay people are victims of an enormous con job, a tragic heist, and it has been going on for too many years. It is time to call its bluff. This means recognizing that we have been here since the beginning of the history of people. It means accepting that men loving men, men having sex with men, has been here since the beginning of history. Every single "case study" quoted by Richard Godbeer (professor of history and gender studies at the University of Miami) knows what I am talking about—and knows why peo-

* Doris Kearns Goodwin is among the most visible and vociferous of our assailants, herself hell-bent on preventing us from claiming Lincoln as one of our own. Goodwin, you will recall, believes Lincoln could not have been gay because lots of men slept in the same bed for four years and wrote love letters full of passion and caring. I wonder if she ever actually saw the bed that Abe and Joshua Speed slept in for four years. It was a very narrow bed, and there's no way that two big men could have slept in it except in each other's arms.

ple didn't write about it in the 18th century. Sodomy was against the law and, depending on the moment in time or place, punishable by death. So of course these guys are not going to write in their letters "An Ode to Your Gorgeous Penis and/or Tush" or the like. Even today, such honesty is rarely available in the "Dear Diary"s of the Great Modern Gays.

In a previous book, Godbeer appears quite willing to entertain the notion that early colonists had active sex lives even in the absence of women. He cites Jamestown as an example and then offers the following: "Settlers in the 17th-century Chesapeake often paired off to form all-male households, living and working together. ... It would be truly remarkable if all the male-only partnerships lacked a sexual ingredient. ... It seems reasonable to assume that much of the sex that took place ... was sodomitical."

In this new book, however, Godbeer is hell-bent on convincing us that two men in colonial America could have exceedingly obsessive and passionate relationships (he calls them, variously, "sentimental," "loving," "romantic") replete with nonstop effusive correspondence that rivals anything in Barbara Cartland, and spend many a night in bed together talking their hearts out, without the issue of sex arising in any way. He tries very hard to convince us that then was so different from now, that men, in essence, in all of this behavior, had no sex drive, indeed no functioning penises that perked up when the luscious emotions and activities one is writing or reading about were experienced. Most of these friendships were not in the least sexual, insists Godbeer—you know, a sort of "I love you, man" for Colonial America.

By the way, many of these young men that Godbeer writes about sound to me like what we used to call weenies, wimps, sissies, wusses—whatever expression you want to use for the guys who never got chosen for the team. There is not a butch or masculine-sounding fellow among them. Read enough of their endless platitudinous meanderings and you'll long for some real men to come along and grab their crotches and plant a deep, long kiss, avec tongue.

Godbeer's early chapters detail young men obsessively in love with each other, wanting to sleep (no sex!) with each other night after night, and often doing so, exchanging that word "love" quite generously. One young man relates a dream in which he pulls his friend out of the water: "he seemed to be stark naked and as we were running along hand in hand to the place where his clothes were—I awakened—greatly agitated by the danger from which we seemed to have escaped." Tormented when apart, greedy for more when together, his lover is "determined we should never part again." "I will give myself up to you, I will go wherever you go and one shall not go without the other." "I love you very much." "Yours for ever—and ever—and ever." These two men were 27 years old.

Godbeer keeps reminding us, as if this explains anything, that there was no word for homosexual back then. To which I reply: so what? Men in love with other men, by this very act alone, knew who they were without having a word for it. And anyway, there were hundreds of words for homosexual. I have a dictionary filled with them—*The Queen's Vernacular* it's called, and it documents centuries of what we called ourselves.

Do you know that men loving men do not require the sexual act to qualify them as homosexuals? My *American Heritage Dictionary* (unabridged) lists two definitions for homosexuality: "sexual orientation to persons of the same sex" and "sexual activity with another of the same sex." By the first of these definitions, every person in Godbeer's book would qualify as homosexual, certainly to me, with or without proof of a consummated sexual act. Just because his research has not uncovered smoking cocks does not mean these loving friendships weren't shooting themselves off all over the thirteen colonies and into the Louisiana Purchase, soon to come. To use Godbeer's own words, it seems reasonable to assume that this would be the case.

How does Godbeer know that most of the intimate friendships he describes were sexually chaste? He has no more evidence to prove his case than do those, like me, who may be quick to discern orgies in colonial beds. The argument goes both ways. If one side cannot wave Monica Lewinsky's semen-stained dress, neither can the other side wave immaculate bed linens.

JUDGING by how much Godbeer quotes from them, much of this romantic friendship stuff appears to have been whipped up by newspapers, of all things, "for the love of one's country." "It would flow outward and transform society as a whole." "It is like a crystal fountain, uncontaminated at its source, issuing its stream along the vale and over the fertile mead, which makes the flowers in spontaneous order spring and flourish, and the valleys smile with pleasure, uniting fragrance over the wide expanse." What upstanding gay man would not respond to this challenge! Go to bed with your best chum and shoot the shit and be an example for all America.

Just because he can't find the hard-core stuff does not mean that same-sex sex did not take place. Even Ron Chernow in *Alexander Hamilton* (2004) and James Gaines in *For Liberty and Glory: Washington, Lafayette, and Their Revolutions* (2007), in laying out all the intertwining relationships between Washington, Hamilton, Lafayette, and John Laurens (Hamilton's great love), admit that they could have all been having sex. Of course, each historian says he doubts it (no reasons given), but at least they admit the possibility, which is a bit of progress. "While there is no irrefutable proof that Laurens and Hamilton were lovers," there is "sufficient circumstantial evidence to render indefensible any unqualified pronouncement that they were not," Godbeer quotes, in a footnote from William Benemann's *Male-Male Intimacy in Early America: Beyond Romantic Friendships*. But Godbeer says, not in a footnote: "Yet we cannot simply assume that men who loved one another must have wanted to have sex." But why not? He offers no explanation, but his book is overflowing with statements of the following kind:

> Figuring out what these romantic friendships meant to people living in the eighteenth century involves setting aside modern assumptions about love between members of the same sex.
>
> The modern assumption that most people are attracted—sexually and romantically—to either men or women would have surprised early Americans.
>
> We know that there were men in British America who found themselves attracted to other men, yet the modern category of "homosexual" would have made little sense to them or their neighbors. ... Strictly speaking, men who practiced sodomy during this period did not engage in homosexual acts, any more than the planter giving his wife "a flourish" was engaging in a heterosexual act.

To all of the above, I cry out: So what? Followed by a resounding: bushwa! What with all those Cotton Mathers and Jonathan Edwardses rushing around ranting about any kind of sex being a sin, I think gay men were probably scared shitless by what they might have been feeling and thinking.

Godbeer even insists that this form of friendship is what made America great: everyone pitching in, showing the world that we're All Together in our hearts and strong, loving, romantic, sentimental, patriotic. Thus, this from Godbeer: "As we will see that spiritual version of male fraternity had radical implications: in the second half of the 18th century, it would combine with the culture of sensibility and the ideology of the American revolution to produce a powerful moral vision for post-revolutionary society that placed love between men at its very center." And this: "It would acquire a particular and explicitly political significance for North Americans during the revolutionary period when the encouragement of intense and loving male friendships came to be seen as crucial to the nation–building project and its creation of worthy republican citizens."

This perfidy is perhaps where Joseph J. Ellis found his notion of Washington, Hamilton, et al. as a band of founding brothers. Well, there is another version of that: George the Father leading his troops into battle by day and, among many other sweet, same-sex deeds, assigning one or another of his favorites to rotate sleeping in his tent at night. Read the great, pioneering, Boston-based gay historian Charley Shively, and you'll never be able to read Joseph J. Ellis (or James McGregor Burns, Douglas Southall Freeman, David McCullough, Arthur Schlesinger, Jr., Edmund S. Morgan, et al.) with a straight face again.

Does Godbeer admit to the possibility that the dark ogre of sex lurks over or inside or under any of this? When he does so, it is grudgingly and in his usual context of doubt:

> Though we should beware of leaping to unwarranted conclusions about the kinds of intimacy that "dear chums" enjoyed when lying "warm" together [why?], it is of course not inconceivable that in some instances "those pleasures" might have included erotic stimulation or even sexual activity. Some letters are a good deal more suggestive than others in expressing nostalgia for nights spent with a close friend. Virgil Maxcy, who lived in Smithfield, Rhode Island, assured his "chum" William Blanding in Rehoboth, Massachusetts, that he missed sleeping with him: "Sometimes," he wrote, "I think I have got hold of your doodle

> when in reality I have hold of the bedpost." A "doodle" that could be confused with a bedpost was hardly in a state of repose, and Maxcy signed this particular letter, "your cunt humble." One cannot help but wonder.

"Cannot help but wonder"? What would it take to convince this guy? This is anemic, sex-panicked, transparently crude obfuscation. The claim that nothing can be said for sure because there are no reliable sources, none of the hard stuff on which historians are supposed to base their accounts, is beginning to wear thin. It is incomprehensible to me how queer theory, gender studies, indeed much of gay history, can continue to get away with making the a priori assumption that these men's sentiments are somehow inaccessible to us, even when it's staring us in the face!

ACTUALLY, the jig might already be up, as an important new book offers a healthy dose of the hard stuff: evidence for same-sex sexual activity in another setting where it has traditionally been denied, namely 19th-century England. Charles Upchurch, an assistant professor of history at Florida State University, has spent ten years researching *Before Wilde: Sex between Men in Britain's Age of Reform* (University of California Press, 2013), and it shows. The book overflows with case after case of hard, irrefutable evidence that English men did with other men pretty much what same-sex couplings do with each other all over the world to this day. The big difference here is that Upchurch begins his extraordinary documentation of these cases in the early 19th century. Upchurch claims to have collected over 1,000 published newspaper articles documenting such cases.

Certainly nothing like this has appeared before in and about America, thus allowing queer and gender studies to pretty much swamp gay history with their gobbledygook theorizing on our inability to know anything definitive about sexual behavior in past eras or to relate it to our own sexual "categories." Well, now it can be said and proved, in Britain at any rate, thanks to this research. Indeed, "an aching gap has been filled," proclaims British sexual theorist Jeffrey Weeks in one of the blurbs on the back cover.

One reads this book with grateful amazement. Here is a scholar, an academic, who has really done his homework. He has read, it would seem, almost every relevant British newspaper and court record from the early 1800s up to about 1870. The amazing thing, of course, when his findings are excavated and exposed to the bright air of daylight, is that all of this information has been there all along—in the files of *The Times* of London, in the court records of cases that it and other newspapers reported, often rather non-judgmentally: cases involving men accused of sodomy or attempted sodomy, of "indecent assault" (at various times punishable by death), of cross-dressing, of hustling, of cruising, of two men trying to set up house or cohabiting in any way—all those things that gay men know all about and take for granted today.

It is breathtaking to read all these accounts in their original context, and on finishing Upchurch's book one heaves a huge sigh of relief. Of course this is how it was! Why did we all not know and accept this instinctively without having to create and buy into the nightmare theories of Michel Foucault and Judith Butler (to name but two) with the obtuse vocabulary they invented to impose their own preconceived order on the real world? To wit: homosexuality did not exist because there was no word for it.

Those days may be fading fast. With more books like *Before Wilde* and more scholars like Upchurch, we might one day even be able to say unapologetically that George Washington and Abraham Lincoln, among others, were our brothers in love.

What's Lost on the Road to Equality

DOLORES KLAICH

WOMEN are marrying women, men are marrying men; many of either persuasion are, with beatific smiles, pushing baby carriages. One's sister, daughter, wife, mother, brother, son, husband, father, grandmother, grandfather, aunt, uncle, colleagues, friends, and neighbors are not just tiptoeing out of the closet but publicly claiming their gayness in all spheres of life. It is, to be sure, a cultural sea change, and one that seems to have happened overnight, at least from the perspective of mainstream America. Who would have imagined such a state of affairs? Certainly not the early gay and lesbian activists of the Stonewall era, those who have now reached a certain age, the folks, along with those who have passed on, who were at the barricades of the early gay liberation movement, years before the alphabet soup of LGBTQ rights. Indeed the shift from "liberation" to "rights," which was a slow morphing over the years, is itself emblematic of what has changed.

Assimilation into the social mainstream has moved steadily apace, and with it have come complications that face all minorities: co-optation, tokenism, paternalism, and a veneer of tolerance. What happened to re-imagining and re-inventing social institutions such as marriage and family, hallmarks of early activist groups? It's astonishing to rediscover the mission statement of New York City's Gay Liberation Front, formed in 1969 following the Stonewall Riots, which included the following self-declaration: "We are a revolutionary group of men and women formed with the realization that complete sexual liberation for all people cannot come about unless existing social institutions are abolished." Can we possibly imagine today's dominant LGBTQ rights organizations describing themselves as "revolutionary" and calling for universal "sexual liberation"?

Gay and lesbian folks who aren't old enough to remember either the bad old days or the early days of gay and lesbian liberation—a growing majority at this time—may be overjoyed that they can partake of the fruits of acceptance (however incomplete) into mainstream society. Most are probably oblivious to the vision of meaningful social change that animated the early activists. Let me consider a few of the major areas in which things have undoubtedly changed, but not quite in the ways that were hoped for when the early movement began.

GAY MARRIAGE. I turn first to an interview with the cult filmmaker John Waters and his much quoted line, "I always thought the privilege of being gay is that we don't have to get married or go into the army." Later in this *New Yorker* interview (March 26, 2007) he proclaimed that marriage, an entrenched heterosexual tradition, was a corny and expensive tradition. Of course gay or lesbian marriages can be more than corny and expensive. Just ask the smart, feisty, hot, cute, charming 83-year-old Edie Windsor [1929–2017] (straight out of central casting), who put the Supreme Court's feet to the fire in 2013 to strike down a monumentally unfair law, the Defense of Marriage Act (DOMA), thus paving the way for state after state to legalize same-sex marriage.

But I wonder: in a country still awash in racism and classism, would an overweight, impoverished woman of color who is lesbian have been as acceptable a plaintiff as was this attractive, wealthy, former IBM executive with a house in the Hamptons? (Full disclosure: Edie is a friend of mine, a kind, loving woman who gives the best hugs around.) One can easily imagine the decision going the other way, which would have been disastrous for lesbians and gay men everywhere. Edie Windsor's undertaking was just plain brave and heroic, and she deserves all the accolades she has garnered. But where in this important scenario is the original vision of the gay, lesbian, and feminist liberation movements, which included a radical agenda of progressive society-wide change, such as a rethinking of the whole institution of marriage, a longing to experiment with a more open-ended, flexible, and varied model for intimate human relationships? As things now stand, one is reminded of the quips by late-night TV hosts when the subject of gay marriage was first in the air: "Sure, I'm all for gay marriage. Why shouldn't they be as miserable as the rest of us?"

THE MILITARY. In 2012, on a military base in Hawaii at a family return-from-duty homecoming celebration, a buff gay Marine—as of September 2011 no longer needing not to tell—planted a passionate kiss and a wildly loving hug onto his boyfriend that in minutes went viral on social media sites. One thinks of Judy Grahn, the lesbian poet and activist who was kicked out of the Air Force for being a lesbian in the early 1960s; or of Lenny Matlovich, the highly decorated Vietnam veteran, also kicked out of the military, who became a gay liberation activist and whose tombstone, carved upon his death in 1988, memorably reads: "When I was in the military, they gave me a medal for killing two men and a discharge for loving one." At the same time, as this quotation poignantly reminds us, the military is a very conservative institution, in times of war a "killing machine," participation in which should be problematical for anyone who questions the legitimacy of war in general and recent American adventures in particular.

PSYCHIATRY. The most recent American attempt to "cure" homosexuals—after thousands of gay men in the U.S. and the U.K. underwent torturous episodes, as documented by historian Martin Duberman in his 1991 book *Cures* and in the recent movie about mathematician Alan Turing, *The Imitation Game*—is the "ex-gay" movement, which emerged a generation ago and continues to this day, albeit showing distinct signs of faltering. In 2012, an influential psychiatrist, Dr. Robert Spitzer, who had claimed in a 2003 study that gay individuals could be "cured" through a method called reparative therapy, admitted that the study, which religious fundamentalists had pounced on to establish "cure" clinics across the country, was "fatally flawed"; and he apologized for promulgating it. He went on to say: "I believe I owe the gay community an apology." Not long after Spitzer's apology, a World Health Organization report called his reparative therapy "a serious threat to the health and well-being—even the lives—of affected people." So here's a case of "assimilation"—into the realm of "normal" psychology—that seems to me an unmixed blessing.

As an aside: the headline in a *New York Times* article about Spitzer's apology (May 18, 2012) read: "Psychiatry Giant Sorry for Backing Gay Cure." To see such a headline in the *Times* attests to a revolution in the *Times'* treatment of gays and lesbians over the past many years. It wasn't until 1987, when the tyrannical, heterosexist executive editor Abe Rosenthal left his post at the paper, that things began to change. Before that, even the word "gay" was banned in favor of the more clinical and subtly pejorative "homosexual"; but since then the *Times* has come to be a reliable and powerful booster for all things gay and lesbian, both in the political and the cultural realms.

BOOKS AND THE ACADEMY. These days, bookstore shelves are groaning with gay- and lesbian-themed books of every description: academic studies, literary and not-so-literary novels, poetry chapbooks, mysteries, memoirs—some of them receiving substantial critical attention (not to mention favorable reviews). This is a far cry from 1973, when a group of Philadelphia activists rented a storefront on the city's South Street to establish a gay and lesbian community gathering place in the hope of including a gay and lesbian bookstore. They named the enterprise Giovanni's Room after the James Baldwin novel and displayed what gay-positive were then available, which filled only one shelf of one short bookcase. However, over the years the bookstore came to thrive, not always financially but as a center of discussion and activism. In 2014, after 41 years as the nucleus of the city's gay and lesbian community, following the fate of many other independent bookstores, Giovanni's Room closed its doors. *Rolling Stone* magazine, in its May 21, 2014, issue, saluted the store and its longtime activist-owner Ed Hermance. When asked about the store's beginnings and its longevity, Hermance said: "We were working on changing the world. That was our motivation."

Moving to the world of academia, one couldn't have imagined a faculty position dedicated to gay and lesbian studies, but in 2009 Harvard University endowed a chair for GLBT studies (the F. O. Matthiessen Visiting Professorship of Gender and Sexuality). But Yale trumped Harvard this time, having failed to endow a similar chair in 1997 but succeeding in 2001. Today, according to College Equality Index, an organization that assists the college search process for prospective LGBT students, there are some forty institutions that offer a minor in LGBT studies (under various names). These victories represent a struggle that started in the 1970s, when graduate students first began to propose topics on gay and lesbian issues in literature and in the social sciences. Even sympathetic faculty members, wary of tenure decisions in their future, would almost always turn their backs on such research. Today, scholars are making up for lost time as doctoral candidates are turning out great numbers of dissertations and books on gay and lesbian topics.

Assimilation into a dominant mainstream has always been a thorny issue for minority groups seeking acceptance. It would be cranky to begrudge the millions of gay men and lesbians who have joyfully embraced mainstream values and norms, even at the cost of jettisoning aspects of their lives that don't fit the mold. But there are still many people who question these values and norms, including those who continue to be on the side of re-envisioning more progressive societal constructs by acting to change the status quo, and those who concur with what James Baldwin wrote in *The Fire Next Time* (with reference to racism): "Do I really want to be integrated into a burning house?"

So, far be it from me or anyone else of a certain age to resent those who are now enjoying the fruits of gay liberation in the form of acceptance into mainstream social institutions. At the same time, these folks should be aware of the inevitable backlash against these gains—anti-gay legislation is afoot in many states as I write—and be prepared to fight back against powerful individuals and groups that seek to destroy what has been gained.

'Homonormativity' and Its Discontents

D. GILSON

WE are leaving the city behind in the dream. We are lying upon the edge of a pool on a cliff overlooking the ocean. In Mexico, the city is behind us and Colby Keller is reading poetry as I float on a raft. Whitman's words were never truer: "We two boys together clinging/ One the other never leaving." On the screen, the scene is fleeting, offering a CockyBoys™ seven-day trial membership for $14.95.

I AM waiting at Dooby's, a hip Baltimore café, for my friend Colby, whom I know quite well digitally, but have yet to meet IRL (in real life). Such is contemporary humanity. Colby Keller is undoubtedly one of the world's biggest gay porn stars, his digital footprint like his bodily footprint, huge, distinct, and instantly recognizable to many. Colby is also one of the smartest—not to mention kindest—men I know; he holds an MFA in sculpture from the Maryland Institute College of Art (MICA), one of the nation's top art schools, and he reads Marxist theory and contemporary poetry voraciously. Here I lay bare a bias: it was initially difficult to reconcile the Colby I knew from his porn, those images of a chiseled Adonis sweating onto the back of a hipster as they fuck, with the Colby that sat across from me, talking of Whitman and what his poetic might mean in the age of neoliberalism.

I met Colby IRL at a time in history, the second decade of the 21st century. Homosexual lobbyists had fought for and were winning a number of new rights, most visibly the ability for homos to serve openly in the military and to marry in a growing number of states (and eventually nationwide). At the same time, I was being drawn into the set of ideas known as queer theory. As luck would have it, the past decade has given rise to an often visceral divide between the academic discipline of queer theory and the mainstream homosexual lobby, represented most prominently by the behemoth Human Rights Campaign. The mainstream homosexual lobby paints academics who criticize them as elitists who are out of touch; queer-minded academics often paint the gay lobby as shortsighted and concerned only with furthering capitalism and its most protected class, white men. To me, Colby Keller has come to be an image, a metaphor, for how these two groups might bridge their aspirations: Colby is a man, after all, visibly concerned with his own sexual desires, but he is also connected to a larger queer politics that recognizes the social needs of others.

IF a thesis here is necessary: Queerness is not threatened most by heteronormativity, but by homonormativity, not by people outside of the LGBT community, but by the most powerful class, white gay men, inside of it. If a theorem here might be helpful to understand the implication of this: queer ≠ gay.

The current definition of "queer" originates with the debate over whether sexuality is "essential" to the person or something that's "socially constructed." Think Lady Gaga's insistence that you're "born this way" versus Michel Foucault's dictum that "the homosexual was now a species" when the word itself was coined. The contemporary homosexual lobby—derided in some corners as "Gay, Inc."—builds its case on essentialism: If we are born this way, then the state cannot discriminate against us. Within state-sanctioned institutions (marriage, the military, taxes), Gay, Inc. finds freedom.

In contrast, "queerness" as a concept is not limited to our individual sexual identities but malleable when describing our politics and ways of thinking about and improving the world. White gay men, who, like white men generally, tend to think they deserve to be on top, find this frustrating, because here queerness might not place their desires first. To many scholars, a gay man could be homosexual without being queer. Believe me, this is not popular to say to drunk dudes grabbing your ass at Pride or to self-righteous, shortsighted guys on Facebook.

David Halperin contends that "Queer is by definition whatever is at odds with the normal, the legitimate, the dominant. There is nothing in particular to which it necessarily refers. It is an identity without an essence." So if a queer politics refers to capacious care for all those at odds with the normal, the legitimate, and the dominant, a queer friendship may be finding that common bond of illegitimacy within the Other. In Colby, for instance, I see a reflection of my anger at mainstream gay politics and, further, the type of ennui I feel at my own comrades' refusal to question such institutions.

QUEER theory as queer politics offers to assemble us into a public, intelligent working group of reformers for issues of race alongside sex and gender. Richard Thompson Ford, in a 2007 article, "What's Queer About Race?," explains his personal excitement to this end:

> Queer theory offered a way to take race politics back from the professionals. It had—at least it seemed to me—a closer and fresher connection with the everyday life of a counterculture, with its contradictions, its sweaty struggles, its passions, its screw-ups, its street styles and fashion faux pas. Queer theory, with its open-handed conflicts and negotiations between gay men, lesbians, trannies, butch and lipstick lesbians, tops, bottoms, clean-shaven Chelsea boys and bearded burly "bears."

This praxis has both political and personal implications, because one of the greatest facets of queer life outside of homonormative gayness is also our ability to define our own relationships.

It is true that sometimes all queer bonding asks for is a recognition, like that between Colby and me, or between Frank O'Hara and his intimate, the painter Grace Hartigan. In a poem to Hartigan, O'Hara surmises this queer recognition: "And someone you love enters the room/ and says wouldn't/ you like the eggs a little/ different today?/ And when they arrive they are/ just plain scrambled eggs."

This desire for plain scrambled eggs is not my way of robbing queerness of sex. I love sex. I have had sex with some of my closest friends. Michel Foucault explains: "A way of life can be shared among individuals of different ages, status, and social activity. It can yield intense relations not resembling those that are institutionalized. It seems to me that a way of life can yield a culture and an ethics. To be 'gay,' I think, is not to identify with the psychological traits and the visible masks of the homosexual but to try and define and develop a way of life."

IN *Tendencies*, Eve Kosofsky Sedgwick contends that "'queer' can refer to: the open mesh of possibilities, gaps, overlaps, dissonances and resonances, lapses and excesses of meaning when the constituent elements of anyone's gender, of anyone's sexuality, aren't made (or can't be made) to signify monolithically." The mainstream gay lobby, representing the most privileged class of queer society, would like us to think of our lives—both our sexual and interpersonal—monolithically; they would like us to act as upstanding straights do in order to gain the rights that in no way should be tied to one's ability to couple or to be "normal."

But surely part of living queerly is giving of oneself to the Other, because, as Judith Butler opines: "Let's face it. We are undone by each other." Butler links desire and grieving, implying that if we can be undone by each other, we can also be radically redone, which is how I've begun to think of my queer friendships, such as my relationships with my best friend Will and with Colby, who in the spring of 2014 undertook an art project titled "Everything But Lenin."

Evicted from his Baltimore studio, Colby decided to leave Charm City, where he had lived for the last decade through graduate school and his rise to porn stardom, to travel the USA. "Everything But Lenin" was his attempt to remove the accumulated possessions from his life, in which he gave away everything but a metal plaque of the Communist icon. Colby understood, as I think many of us suspect, that things have the ability to possess us just as much as, perhaps more than, we have the ability to possess them.

Butler speaks of our gender and sexuality as things, positing that "neither of these is precisely a possession, but both are to be understood as modes of being dispossessed, ways of being for another, or indeed, by virtue of another." If gayness is a thing we can both know and possess through legislation and through the accumulation of shiny, glittery things, then perhaps queerness is that which we can never know, the thing that, every day, can dispossess us from ourselves. In this way we are undone and redone ad infinitum.

Outside of academia and far-Left activism, "queer" has become generally synonymous with "gay." Linguistically, this may be dangerous because the contemporary gay lobby puts forward a very narrow definition of what is acceptable gayness, which they call queerness, but is anything but. Which is to say, to be gay in the 21st century is to be a white, wealthy, urban, cisgendered man. By this reasoning, the gay man of today is often not unlike the conservative man: concerned first for his own needs and second for the needs of normal members of society.

A DUAL phenomenon exists in how we raise gay boys, as both group victim and individual phenomenon. From the current focus on the bullying of LGBT children and teens, a discourse of "You are not alone!" has arisen. This is most prominently vocalized through Dan Savage's "It Gets Better" campaign, which, intentionally or not, is focused primarily on the needs of upwardly mobile white youth, gay teens like those on *Glee*—the type of angst-ridden boy that I was. The campaign's rationale goes something like this: "Dear gay boy: Don't worry. Some day you will move to a big city and be surrounded by other fabulous gay men with law degrees and jobs in finance. The world will be yours."

Conversely, we live in a parenting culture that tells all children they deserve a trophy for being unique, special, one-of-a-kind snowflakes. My sister is a reading specialist for a school district in southern Missouri, and on a recent trip home I visited her classroom one afternoon. Atop every desk, a ribbon was taped; onto these ribbons my sister had hand-painted various designations: "Best Finder of Verbs," "Best Listener," "Best Helper at Afternoon Snack Time." She changes these biweekly, creating new categories and, she admitted to me, often struggling to think of something that each child is "best at." Her practice here is more than a little neurotic, but it is also indicative of a culture wanting to believe that every child is above average, which is impossible, with the potential for true excellence, which is simply not true.

Young gay boys, who become gay men, are constantly told they are both a unique snowflake and part of a victimized group. The result is an army of gay men allowed to be simultaneously powerbroker and victim. Put another way, the result is the typical, entitled gay man one might encounter in Washington, D.C.

TO live in Washington is to learn the technique of avoidance. My office sits at the corner of 22nd and I Streets NW, an intersection at the heart of George Washington University, frequented by nonprofit canvassers. Colleagues and I avoid walking by these people if possible, which it rarely is, or at least avoid engaging with them as we rush by, not listening to whatever cause they're selling. The Human Rights Campaign (HRC) keeps a steady stream of "fundraising associates" at this intersection, mostly young gay men who think working for the HRC buys some credibility, and young women who look like they were dressed by their gay male colleagues.

Recently a cute guy asked if I wanted to become an HRC member as I walked from office to Metro. "No, sorry," I said, but he jogged to catch up: "Do you not care about gay rights?" I stopped and in no uncertain terms, barked a treatise on why the HRC does not represent my political interests or those of a queer politic writ large. Their politicking for most of the past decade has centered primarily on three issues: 1) the overturning of "Don't ask, don't tell," thus allowing gays to serve openly in the U.S. military, i.e., an intrinsically homophobic war machine whose very existence should be open to debate; 2) the expansion of state-sanctioned marriage to gay and lesbian couples on both the state and national level, which invites the government to enter into their relationships with the promise of certain benefits such as health care and tax breaks, which should be available to everyone; and 3) the ranking of companies as "gay friendly" on an annual "Corporate Equality Index."

This last project drives me bat-shit crazy, as it labels otherwise horrible multinational corporations as stellar places for gays to work. The HRC's 2015 list includes oil companies that are wreaking havoc on the environment (Chevron, Exxon-Mobil); pharmaceutical companies more concerned with inflated profits than providing essential medicines to the sick and suffering (GlaxoSmithKline, Pfizer); defense companies developing weapons that allow the U.S. and its allies to take over countries and their resources (Lockheed Martin, Northrop Grumman); financial conglomerates that caused the 2008 global economic crisis and used subsequent public bailouts to pay bonuses to already overcompensated executives (Goldman Sachs, JPMorgan Chase); and finally, because of its political maneuvering and takeover of the world's farming and food, the one that many regard as the most evil corporation on the face of the earth: Monsanto. And yet, because these companies train employees in diversity, or give partner benefits, or financially support the gay rights lobby, they are deemed the best places for us to work.

I DREAM of Colby reading Whitman, twisting beard between forefinger and thumb: "I will plant companionship thick as trees along all the rivers of America, and along the shores of the great lakes, and all over the prairies, / I will make inseparable cities with their arms about each other's necks, / By the love of comrades, / By the manly love of comrades."

I dream of a Queer America, which is why I want Colby Keller to run for president. My friend embodies queerness; he does not rob it of sex, as the political Right would do; nor does he rob it of a capaciously queer, revolutionary politic, as the mainstream gay lobby would do, asking us not to question capitalism, or consumerism, or militarism, but instead to accept these on our path to homonormativity. I can imagine Colby, perhaps clad in cowboy hat and chaps, reading from the "Queer Nation Manifesto" at a campaign rally:

> Being queer means leading a different sort of life. It's not about the mainstream, profit margins, patriotism, patriarchy, or being assimilated. It's not about executive directors, privilege and elitism. It's about being on the margins, defining ourselves; it's about gender-fuck and secrets, what's beneath the belt and deep inside the heart; it's about the night. Being queer is "grass roots" because we know that every one of us, every body, every cunt, every heart and ass and dick is a world of pleasure waiting to be explored. Everyone of us is a world of infinite possibility.

To repeat: we live in a time when queerness is not threatened most by heteronormativity, but by homonormativity. But every one of us is a world of infinite possibility.

Contributors

DENNIS ALTMAN is the author of *Homosexual: Oppression and Liberation* (1971), *The Homosexualization of America* (1982), and *Global Sex* (2001), among other books. He is a professorial fellow at La Trobe University in Australia.

DAVID B. BOYCE (1949–2014), a freelance art critic and longtime curatorial consultant at the New Bedford Art Museum, was a model for one of the men in the statue *Gay Liberation* in Christopher Park in New York's West Village.

MICHAEL BRONSKI, author of *Culture Clash* (1984) and numerous other books, including *A Queer History of the United States for Young People* (2019), is Professor of the Practice in Activism and Media in Studies of Women, Gender and Sexuality at Harvard University.

FRANK BROWNING, a longtime correspondent for NPR, is the author of *The Culture of Desire: Paradox and Perversity in Gay Lives Today* (1993) and *The Fate of Gender: Nature, Nurture, and the Human Future* (2016).

DAVID CARTER is the author of *Stonewall: The Riots That Sparked the Gay Revolution* (2004), which was later adapted as a PBS documentary titled "Stonewall Uprising" (2010) for the *American Experience* series.

STEVEN F. DANSKY has been an activist, documentarian, photographer, and writer for more than fifty years.

JOHN D'EMILIO, recently retired professor of history at the University of Illinois at Chicago, is the author of *Sexual Politics, Sexual Communities: The Making of a Homosexual Minority in the United States, 1940-1970* (1998) and *Lost Prophet: The Life and Times of Bayard Rustin* (2003), among other books.

MICHAEL DENNENY, a co-founder of *Christopher Street* magazine in 1976, worked as a senior editor and published numerous gay books at St. Martin's Press starting in the 1980s. He currently works as an independent editor in New York City.

MARTIN DUBERMAN is the author of *Stonewall* (1994), *The Worlds of Lincoln Kirstein* (2007), and *Luminous Traitor: The Just and Daring Life of Roger Casement* (2018), among many other books. Founder of the Center for Gay and Lesbian Studies at CUNY, he was professor of history at Lehman College for many years.

LILLIAN FADERMAN, author of *Surpassing the Love of Men: Romantic Friendship and Love Between Women from the Renaissance to the Present* (1981), *Odd Girls and Twilight Lovers: A History of Lesbian Life in Twentieth-Century America* (1991), and *The Gay Revolution: The Story of the Struggle* (2015), taught history at California State–Fresno until 2007.

D. GILSON, author of *I Will Say This Exactly One Time: Essays* (2015) and (with Will Stockton) *Crush* (2014), is an assistant professor of English at the Massachusetts College of Liberal Arts.

EVE GOLDBERG is a writer and filmmaker who lives in northern California. Her films include *Kids of Survival* (1996) and the short documentary "Lori and Cathy Get Married" (2005).

JEWELLE GOMEZ, a writer and playwright who's known as the "foremother of Afrofuturism," is the author of *The Gilda Stories* (1991; Expanded Edition in 2016) and other books. Her stories have been anthologized in over 100 collections.

HARRY HAY (1912–2002) was an early gay activist who founded the Mattachine Society in Los Angeles in 1948 and was one of the organizers of the Radical Faeries in the 1970s.

AMY HOFFMAN is the author of the novel *The Off Season* and the memoirs *Hospital Time, An Army of Ex-Lovers: My Life at the Gay Community News,* and *Lies About My Family*. A writing instructor at Emerson College, she was editor-in-chief of *Women's Review of Books* for fourteen years.

ANDREW HOLLERAN, who has contributed to nearly every issue of *The G&LR* since 1994, is the author of the novels *Dancer from the Dance* (1978), *Nights in Aruba* (1983), *The Beauty of Men* (1996), and *Grief* (2006).

KARLA JAY, professor emerita of English, Women's and Gender Studies, and Queer Studies at Pace University in New York, is the author of *Tales of the Lavender Menace* (1999), a memoir about creating the modern LGBT movement in the wake of the Stonewall uprising.

JILL JOHNSTON (1929–2010) was a writer for *The Village Voice*, mostly as a dance critic, for many years. She is the author of the book *Lesbian Nation: The Feminist Solution* (1973), which advocated lesbian-feminist separatism.

ARNIE KANTROWITZ, longtime gay activist who was one of the early founders of the Gay Activists Alliance in 1970, is the author of *Under the Rainbow: Growing Up Gay* (1977) and *Walt Whitman* ("Gay and Lesbian Writers" series, 2005).

DOLORES KLAICH is the author of *Woman + Woman: Attitudes Toward Lesbianism* (1974) and the detective novel *Heavy Gilt* (1988).

LARRY KRAMER is a screenwriter (*Women in Love*), playwright (*The Normal Heart*), bestselling novelist (*Faggots*), and gay and AIDS activist (co-founder of the Gay Men's Health Crisis and founder of ACT UP). Volume One of his latest novel, *The American People* (2015), will soon be joined by Volume Two.

TOBY MAROTTA is the author of *The Politics of Homosexuality* (1981) and *Sons of Harvard: Gay Men from the Class of 1967* (1982).

DEL MARTIN (1921–2008) and PHYLLIS LYON (b. 1924), lifelong partners who were married in 2004, were the major founders of the lesbian organization the Daughters of Bilitis, in San Francisco, in 1955.

FELICE PICANO is a writer whose fiction includes *The Lure* (1979), *Like People in History* (1995), *Onyx* (2001), and the forthcoming *Justify My Sins* (2019). Among his several memoirs are *Ambidextrous: The Secret Lives of Children* (1985) and *Nights at Rizzoli* (2014).

JOHN RECHY is the author of *City of Night* (1963) and numerous other novels, including his most recent work, *After the Blue Hour* (2017).

WILL ROSCOE, PHD, is the author of *The Zuni Man-Woman* (1991) and *Jesus and the Shamanic Tradition of Same-Sex Love* (2004), both of which received Lambda Literary Awards.

Ellen Shumsky was a founding member of the Radicalesbians and co-author of the manifesto "The Woman-Identified Woman" (1970). Her photographs were collected in *Portrait of a Decade (1968–1978)* in 2009.

Bob Smith (1958–2018) was a stand-up comedian and writer who toured as one of the three Funny Gay Males in the 1990s and was the first openly gay comedian to perform on *The Tonight Show*.

Timothy Stewart-Winter, author of *Queer Clout: Chicago and the Rise of Gay Politics* (2016), is an associate professor of history at Rutgers University–Newark.

Martha E. Stone is the literary editor of *The Gay & Lesbian Review* and has written for virtually every issue since the magazine's inception.

Edmund White is the author of the novels *A Boy's Own Story* (1982), *The Beautiful Room Is Empty* (1988), and *The Farewell Symphony* (1997), among many others; nonfiction works including biographies of Marcel Proust and Jean Genet; and the recent memoir *The Unpunished Vice: A Life of Reading* (2018).

Acknowledgements

Special thanks to the following individuals who helped make this book possible: Martha E. Stone, for help with content selection and copy editing; Stephen Hemrick, for managing production, distribution, and marketing; Michael Schwartz and Jim Farley, for copy editing; Charles Hefling, for illustrations and art consultation; and the *G&LR* Board of Directors, whose names appear below, for encouraging this project and for supporting the magazine throughout the year.